POVERTY IN EUROPE

𝕁𝔹

Yrjö Jahnsson was Professor of Economics at the Helsinki University of Technology between 1911 and 1936. In 1954, his wife Hilma Jahnsson established, in accordance with her late husband's wishes, the Yrjö Jahnsson Foundation. The purpose of the Foundation is to promote Finnish research in economics and medical science, and to support Finnish institutions of research and education.

In the field of economics the Foundation is the most important source of private research funding in Finland. It supports the work of individual scholars and institutes by awarding them scholarships and grants. It organizes scientific seminars and workshops in the field of economics and medicine. And it invites internationally renowned economists to Finland to give lectures.

In 1963 the Foundation launched a special series of the Yrjö Jahnsson Lectures, which are organized in Helsinki every two or three years and which are published. Up to the end of 1996 no fewer than five of the economists who have served as lecturers in this series have been awarded the Nobel Prize in economics.

THE YRJÖ JAHNSSON LECTURES

Kenneth J. Arrow
Aspects of the Theory of Risk-Bearing

Assar Lindbeck
Monetary-Fiscal Analysis and General Equilibrium

L. R. Klein
An Essay on the Theory of Economic Prediction

Harry G. Johnson
The Two-Sector Model of General Equilibrium

John Hicks
The Crisis in Keynesian Economics

Edmond Malinvaud
The Theory of Unemployment Reconsidered

James Tobin
Asset Accumulation and Economic Activity

János Kornai
Growth, Shortage and Efficiency

Jacques H. Drèze
Labour Management, Contracts and Capital Markets

Robert E. Lucas
Models of Business Cycles

Amartya Sen
Rational Behaviour

A. B. Atkinson
Poverty in Europe

YRJÖ JAHNSSON LECTURES

Poverty in Europe

A. B. Atkinson

First published 1998

2 4 6 8 10 9 7 5 3 1

Blackwell Publishers Ltd
108 Cowley Road
Oxford OX4 1JF
UK

Blackwell Publishers Inc.
350 Main Street
Malden, Massachusetts 02148
USA

British Library Cataloguing in Publication Data

A CIP catalogue record for this book is available from the
British Library.

Library of Congress Cataloging-in-Publication Data

Atkinson, A. B. (Anthony Barnes)
    Poverty in Europe / A.B. Atkinson.
        p.   cm. — (Yrjö Jahnsson lectures)
    Includes bibliographical references and index.
    ISBN 0-631-20909-3 (hardbound). — ISBN 0-631-21029-6 (pbk.)
    1. Poverty—European Union countries. 2. European Union
countries—Economic policy. I. Title. II. Series.
HC240.9.P6A85   1998
339.4'6'094—dc21   98-11439
                                                                CIP

Typeset in 10 on 11 pt Times New Roman
by Ace Filmsetting Ltd, Frome, Somerset
Printed in Great Britain by MPG Books, Bodmin, Cornwall

This book is printed on acid-free paper.

Contents

INTRODUCTION   1
Poverty in Rich Countries

World poverty and poverty in rich countries. Introduction to European Commission (EC) definition of poverty (50 per cent average income in Member State) and estimates of poverty in Europe in late 1980s. Structure of three Lectures.

LECTURE 1   10
Political Arithmetic: Financial Poverty in the European Union

Definition and measurement of poverty in Europe.

1.1 The Measurement of Poverty: Two Cautionary Tales   10
Comparison of poverty in France and the United Kingdom in 1985. Different interpretations of 50 per cent average income as poverty standard, leading to different conclusions about relative poverty rates. A Pessimist's and an Optimist's views as to whether poverty is increasing in Ireland.

[v]

Figures and their Sources

[ix]

Tables

Preface

This book contains a revised version of the material presented as the twelfth Yrjö Jahnsson Lectures at the University of Helsinki in March 1990. I was very honoured by the invitation to lecture in this famous series, towards which I felt considerable warmth ever since as a student I read the celebrated lectures by Kenneth Arrow on *Aspects of the Theory of Risk-Bearing*. The topic which I chose for the Lectures has also a connection with my student days, since one of the reasons why I switched from studying mathematics to economics was a concern about the persistence of poverty in rich countries. In this respect, I hope that my choice of subject is an appropriate one, in that I note from the history of the Foundation by Seppo Zetterberg (1984) that:

> In his student days Yrjö Jahnsson also joined social reformist movement, which sought to improve the position of the poor. (1984, p. 9)

This book may not directly achieve that aim, but I hope that it will enhance our understanding of the problem of poverty in Europe, and hence contribute to an improvement in policy.

The subject matter of the Lectures is wide-ranging, and I could not hope to compress into three hours an adequate coverage of all of the many different questions which are raised by considering poverty in Europe. I covered only a selection, and this is equally true of the written version. I have retained a three-lecture format, and the book makes no pretence to give a comprehensive treatment. While I have elaborated a number of aspects in the written version, there are many important omissions, for which I apologize. I apologize also to the Foundation for the long delay in producing this final text. The delay has meant, however, that the book is better than it otherwise would have been, since a great deal of relevant research has been published, on which I have been able to draw. (And, of course, Finland has joined the European Union.) I hope that this is some compensation, although I have been unable to include full reference to the Eurostat study of poverty (Eurostat, 1997) which was published as the manuscript was being finalized for press.

In revising the Lectures I have benefitted from the comments made in Helsinki, including the seminar organized by Professor J. Paunio at the University of Helsinki. I have drawn extensively on research carried out with others, and I am grateful to Sandrine Cazes, Karen Gardiner, Valérie Lechene and Holly Sutherland, for allowing me to draw on our joint work. I have also benefitted a great deal from the collaboration in the European Community Human Capital and Mobility Programme Network on Comparative Social Policy and Taxation Modelling, and I thank François Bourguignon, Andrea Brandolini, Louis Chauvel, Danièle Meulders, Brian Nolan, Nicola Rossi and Aino Salomäki for their help with information about their own countries. The February 1997 version of the manuscript has been read by Andrea Brandolini, Karen Gardiner, Richard Hauser, John Hills, Valérie Lechene, Brian Nolan, Martin Ravallion and Holly Sutherland. All of them made very helpful comments, which have allowed me to make significant improvements. Judith Atkinson helped me with the bibliography and Sarah Atkinson with the index. I am most grateful for comments from Seppo Honkapohja of the University of Helsinki, who referred the draft to Saku Aura, and to Markus Jäntti and Veli-Matti Ritakallio for more recent Finnish data. None of the above are, however, in any way responsible for errors or for the views expressed, with which in some cases they disagree!

Finally, I would like to thank Jaakko Kiander, Seppo Honkapohja and the Yrjö Jahnsson Foundation for the hospitality I received during my visit to Helsinki.

A. B. Atkinson
September 1997

Introduction
Poverty in Rich Countries

April 1997 saw a headline in the *Guardian* newspaper, 'Children in poverty: Britain tops the European league' (28 April 1997). Should we be concerned about this 'damaging report'? For two groups of people the answer is 'no'. First, there are those who are not the slightest troubled about poverty, nor about social exclusion. This book is not for them – unless they are willing to suspend their lack of concern. Second, there are those who question whether it makes sense to talk about poverty in rich countries, given the much more pressing problems on a world scale? In the study cited by the *Guardian*, Eurostat used as a poverty line an amount equal to half average income in Member States. However, does it make any sense to take a poverty line in Europe which is twice the average income in Ecuador (where per capita income is approximately a quarter that in the European Union)? Or seven and a half times that in Nigeria?[1]

The relation between world poverty and poverty in rich countries is a difficult question, and I am far from sure that I have a fully satisfactory answer, but it seems to me that there are two important elements in distinguishing these concerns. The first is a matter of the order of priority. I would certainly agree that the problems of the Sahel are more pressing than those addressed in these Lectures. But this does not mean that the issue of poverty in Britain is unimportant. What I am suggesting is a lexicographic ordering of objectives. World poverty has priority, but poverty within rich countries may legitimately come next on our list of concerns. Even if all ships in reach of the *Titanic* had an overriding obligation to steam to its

1 These figures are based on purchasing power parity estimates of GNP per capita from the World Bank (1996, table 1, pp. 188–9).

rescue, this does not mean that they should not have taken steps to protect their steerage passengers from exposure.

The second element in my answer focuses on the geographical scope of the definition. Whereas efforts to reduce world poverty arise from a concern with human survival which knows no frontiers, policy towards poverty in rich countries is defined with respect to a specified population: the poverty line is explicitly drawn with respect to a particular place and time. The concept of social exclusion, which has come to be used widely in conjunction with the European debate about poverty, relates to a specified society. It is concerned with the relation between people and the community in which they live. This is not to suggest that poverty of the first type is confined to poor countries. Physical survival is an issue for people in OECD countries. One has only to think of those living on the streets of our cities. I personally find it very distressing that this has increased rather than decreased in the past decades. It is a shameful indictment of our society that the twentieth century should end, just as it began, with people begging on the streets of Oxford. At the same time, I am concerned about people whose physical survival is assured but who by the standards of the community are judged to be poor and who are excluded from full participation in their society.

This book is for those who accept that economic, or financial, poverty in Europe is a legitimate concern. That such concern exists is evidenced by official statements.

The European Commission has taken an active role in the development of measures of poverty in Europe. In the evaluation report of December 1981 on the first European Action Programme to combat poverty, the European Commission (1981) made an estimate of 36.8 million poor people in the Community (of 12 countries) in 1975, using the half average income poverty criterion described above. This criterion was the concrete implementation of the definition adopted by the Council of Ministers of

> persons whose resources (material, cultural and social) are so limited as to exclude them from the minimum acceptable way of life in the Member State in which they live. (Council Decision, 19 December 1984)

Subsequently, the Interim Report on the Second European Poverty Programme (European Commission, 1989), based on the work of O'Higgins and Jenkins (1990), estimated that the number of poor had increased from 38 million in 1975 to 44 million in 1985. The Final Report on the Second Programme, taking expenditure rather than income as the indicator of resources, reached the alternative estimate for 1985 of 50 million people (see Eurostat, 1990). (The *Guardian* article cited at the beginning of the Introduction referred to the more recent Eurostat (1997) study for 1993, which showed 57 million with incomes below the poverty line in that year.)

The estimates made by the European Commission of the number of people living in financial poverty in Europe have played a powerful role in ensuring public and political support for the extension of the social responsibilities of the Community. The function of the statistics in this case is to *mobilize* policy. Looking to the future, a definition of poverty is necessary in monitoring any increased need for social protection, as a result of the development of the Internal Market and of Monetary Union. Poverty statistics may also be used in the *execution* of policy. The incidence of low incomes may be used to identify sub-groups of the population, such as the elderly or lone parents, where policy initiatives are required. Just as unemployment rates are used in determining the need for labour market intervention, so too poverty rates by region may be used in the allocation of the Social Fund or other Community programmes.

The statistics do, however, raise a number of questions – questions which may in turn give rise to doubts as to whether they are sufficiently firmly based to provide an accurate instrument for monitoring the evolution of poverty in Europe and for policy decisions. With application to policy execution, issues of comparability across member states become particularly important. The use of such an indic-ator to allocate Community funds may provide national or local governments with an incentive to over-state the degree of poverty, counterbalancing their natural political desire to minimize the extent of the problem.

Lecture 1

The first Lecture is concerned with the extent of financial poverty in the European Union and the trend in recent years. (The terms 'economic poverty' and 'financial poverty' are used interchangeably in this book; in many cases I refer simply to 'poverty', but it is the economic/financial dimension that I have in mind.) In order to obtain Union-wide figures, and to make comparisons between Member States, it is necessary to have sources and methods that are comparable. The Community estimate of 50 million is based on the same kind of source – household budget surveys – but these surveys themselves vary across countries and they are analysed in different ways. The posing of the survey questions may differ across countries and the same questions may have different connotations in different social and economic contexts. There are variations in the methods of analysis, including, for example, the procedures for grossing-up for

[3]

differential non-response, or for the omission of atypical households, or for the treatment of durable expenditure. Lecture 1 begins with two cautionary tales about the sensitivity of poverty estimates to the methods used in their construction – a warning that matters of definition are not to be left purely to footnotes, or to economists!

Solid basis for the 50 million figure[2] is provided by the study carried out by the late Aldi Hagenaars, together with Klaas de Vos and Asghar Zaidi (1994) for Eurostat, using household expenditure as the indicator of financial poverty. A small selection of their rich results is presented in Table 0.1, showing the proportion of the population in each Member State below 50 per cent of the mean expenditure for the country in which they live. The countries are ranked in descending order of the poverty per centage. Figure 0.1 is a map of poverty in Europe. The countries with high proportions of their populations below the poverty line tend to be in Southern Europe. However,

Table 0.1   Estimates of poverty rates in the European Community in the late 1980s

	number of persons (thousands)	Percentage
Portugal (1989)	2,525	24.5
Italy	12,111	21.1
Greece	1,868	18.7
Spain	6,546	16.9
Ireland (1987)	556	15.7
United Kingdom	8,436	14.8
France (1989)	8,234	14.7
Luxembourg (1987)	41	11.1
Germany (West)	6,675	10.9
Belgium	729	7.4
Netherlands	706	4.8
Denmark (1987)	200	3.9
TOTAL EUR12	48,628	15.0

Source: Hagenaars et al. (1994, table 3.2).
Note: Figures relate to 1988 unless otherwise indicated.

2 The emphasis in these Lectures on this figure is a source of some embarrassment in that it excludes the three European Union countries which were not members of the then Community: Austria, Finland and Sweden. But as will become evident, even this degree of cross-country comparison is difficult to achieve in the present state of knowledge.

[4]

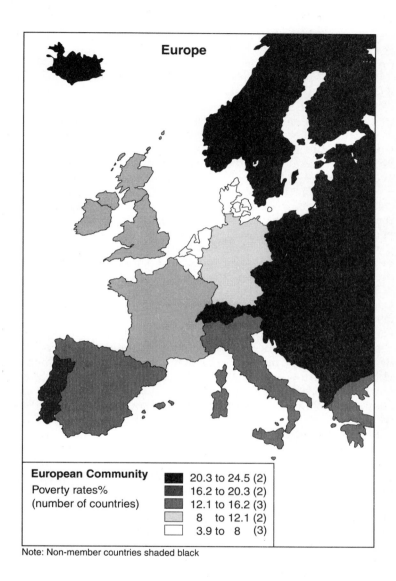

Europe

European Community
Poverty rates%
(number of countries)

■ 20.3 to 24.5 (2)
■ 16.2 to 20.3 (2)
■ 12.1 to 16.2 (3)
□ 8   to 12.1 (2)
□ 3.9 to 8   (3)

Note: Non-member countries shaded black

Figure 0.1 Map of poverty in the
European Community in the late 1980s.
Source: Hagenaars et al. (1994, table 3.2).

poverty is not just a matter for the less well-off countries. About two-thirds of the 50 million are to be found in France, Italy, West Germany and the United Kingdom.

These statistics of poverty in the European Community raise fundamental questions, and a selection are examined in sections 1.2–1.4 of Lecture 1. Is it the case, as some British politicians have suggested, that the measurement of poverty is nothing other than the measurement of inequality by another name? If poverty can be distinguished from inequality and significance attached to a particular poverty line, how is the choice of a relative poverty line – like the 50 per cent of average income – to be justified? Should we not be using an absolute poverty line? The Commission in the estimates just quoted, in contrast to its earlier practice, takes expenditure, rather than income, as the indicator of resources. What arguments are there for using expenditure? If it is income, should it be the income of the household as a whole, or of individual members assessed separately? Is the *number* of people in poverty our sole concern, or should we try to measure the *severity* of poverty?

The European Commission is not the only source of evidence about poverty in Member States. In section 1.5, I summarize some of the evidence from national studies of poverty, drawing on both official and academic sources. These national studies are not directly comparable one with another, but they allow us to investigate the way in which poverty is changing over time in the different Member States. Have the macro-economic events of the past 15 years led to a large increase in measured poverty? They also allow us to see how many people live below the legal minimum set by social security in different countries.

It should be stressed at the outset that the information available about poverty in Europe is limited in scope and in quality. It should be borne in mind that figures may have a sizeable sampling error and may fluctuate from year to year for other reasons (such as variation in agricultural incomes). In particular, the estimates relate to the population living in households, and hence exclude those living in institutions and the homeless. Some of the most deprived members of the Community are therefore missing from the statistics.

Lecture 2

If the figures for poverty In Europe have validity, then they raise serious questions for those concerned with the social dimension of Europe. Why is it that poverty persists in rich European countries? How is the extent of poverty related to economic structure and the working of labour and product markets? What is the role of high unemployment? Why have welfare states not abolished poverty? Do we need to reform the system of social transfers?

In Lecture 2, I ask what light can be cast by economic analysis on the conceptual issues which arise in the definition of poverty and how it can help us understand its persistence. A unifying theme is the three-way relation between poverty, unemployment and the concept of social exclusion. In considering the economic causes of poverty in Europe in the 1990s, one thinks immediately of unemployment, and this is the subject of sections 2.1 and 2.2. I first examine the relation between macro-economic policy (inflation and unemployment) and poverty. Evidence for the United States indicated that a fall in unemployment could be expected to lead to a fall in poverty, but this may have changed with the expansion of the 1980s, and the European experience is more mixed. The relationship between macro-economic variables and poverty is a complex one. While unemployment may lead to poverty, it does not necessarily do so, and poverty may increase without any rise in unemployment. Unemployment may generate not only poverty but also *social exclusion*. Social exclusion is a term which carries many different connotations and there does not seem to be agreement as to how it should be interpreted in a European Union context. In part it is undoubtedly social, rather than economic, in content, but there is an economic dimension, which I seek to illuminate. In section 2.2, I explore the implications of a range of models of unemployment. While I acknowledge the importance of non-economic considerations, I argue that economics has some useful things to say, particularly about the mechanisms which cause people to be excluded. Attention tends to be focused on the victims themselves as the causes of exclusion ('blaming the victim'), whereas it may be the actions of others, and the structures of markets and state intervention, which produce exclusion.

Exclusion is not confined to the labour market, and the second part of the Lecture (sections 2.3 and 2.4) uses the theory of industrial economics to cast light on exclusion from consumption. People may not be able to participate in a consumption activity because the prices charged exclude them from the market. An example would be the fixed tariff charged by electricity companies. This means that we have to look at the determinants of pricing policy. The conditions under which goods are supplied is an aspect which is overlooked in the analysis of poverty. People may equally be excluded because the products which they used to buy are no longer available. The poor cannot, for example, find cheaper cuts of meat or small quantities. Goods are supplied with expensive packaging. Again these decisions are made by suppliers. The model presented is that of a monopoly supplier, but there is no guarantee that competition will ensure that a full range of products are available in the market. The results of the model have implications for public policy, such as the regulation of utilities, and for the adjustment over time of the poverty line.

Decision-making by households is developed further in section 2.5, which explores the treatment of household production in terms of activities which require inputs of both goods and time. The model is applied to the problem of the incomplete take-up of means-tested benefit, a situation in which the benefit system itself is exclusionary. This is one of the reasons why people are living below the legal minimum in European countries.

Lecture 3

Governments profess to have as their objective the alleviation of poverty. Lecture 3 deals with the political economy of anti-poverty policy. In part it is directed at the better design of such policies. Can we ensure that the poorest are protected against the rigours of macro-economic adjustment? Does the solution lie in better targeting of benefits? Can there be a concerted European effort to reduce poverty? But we have also to recognize that past policies have failed to eradicate poverty. We have therefore to be concerned with the analysis of poverty itself: the political economy of anti-poverty policy.

The first section (section 3.1) asks the question – what difference does it make to have an official poverty line? The existence of an official line (as in the United States) is often taken for granted, but how concretely does it affect policy? What is the impact of the European Commission 50 per cent of average poverty line? In order to explore these questions, I consider the theory of economic policy – both old-style and new-style – and its application to anti-poverty policy.

Viewed in a macro-economic light, there appears to be an inevitable tension between reducing poverty and achieving macro-economic stability, anti-poverty policy involving additional public spending, in flat opposition to the Maastricht criteria. Contemplation of this dilemma has led to enthusiasm for better targeting of social transfers. Redirection of transfers, it is claimed, allows them to both cheaper and more effective. Targeting and efficiency in the alleviation of poverty are the subject of section 3.2.

There are, however, a number of problems with this approach. The scope for effective targeting is limited by administrative factors, by the impact on economic incentives, and by considerations of political economy, as is argued in section 3.3. If targeting does not offer a resolution of the dilemma, are there are other paths which could be followed by welfare states in Europe? In order to explore this, we need to consider more fully the interrelation between social and economic policies, and the nature of the fiscal constraints. In section 3.4, I ask whether there is any scope for seeking to establish an effective European minimum which is consistent with Europe's other objectives; and, in section 3.5, I consider the form of such a European minimum.

Warning

The analysis of social policy presented here is undoubtedly influenced by the United Kingdom viewpoint from which I write. Historically, social protection has developed in different ways in different European countries. The Nordic tradition is different from that found in, say, Germany, and the German system in turn differs from that in the United Kingdom. The resulting systems are, moreover, a complex combination of different elements, and cannot readily be classified under the heading of 'ideal types'. In substance, UK policy over the 1980s and early 1990s went much further towards cutting back the welfare state than the rest of the European Union. The conclusions reached regarding the limits of targeting reflect this experience. The reader should bear in mind this insularity of perspective.

Lecture 1

Political Arithmetic: Financial Poverty in the European Union

---

The first Lecture is about the measurement of financial poverty in the European Union. As such, it is concerned with conceptual, definitional and statistical issues.[1] These issues are important since poverty statistics play a significant political role, as reflected in the first part of the title for this Lecture, which is taken from Sir William Petty, whose seventeenth-century *Political Arithmetick* (1676) was a pioneering attempt to base public policy on quantitative evidence. It is also particularly appropriate to the first section in that he was much concerned with the comparison of Britain and France,[2] the first of two cautionary tales about the measurement of poverty with which I begin.

1.1 The Measurement of Poverty: Two Cautionary Tales

The reader may think that definitional issues are in reality of limited practical importance; that they are the theoretical niceties of an academic far-removed from personal experience either of poverty or of anti-poverty policy. Yet the statistical implementation of poverty measures demonstrates that matters of definition may significantly

1 Among the recent surveys of the conceptual issues are Callan and Nolan (1991), Ravallion (1992), Förster (1993) and the Report of the United States National Academy of Sciences Panel on Poverty and Family Assistance (Citro and Michael, 1995). Poverty on a global scale is reviewed by Townsend (1993) and Øyen et al. (1996).
2 One of his ten Principal Conclusions was that: 'the people and territories of the King of England, are naturally near as considerable, for wealth and strength, as those of France'.

affect the conclusions drawn. A government aiming to find a small percentage below a specified poverty line can, by judicious choice of definition, arrive at a dramatically different figure from that reached on another set of definitions. Changes in definition can lead us to have a quite different view of the causes of poverty through their effects on the measured composition of the population defined to be below the poverty line. On one definition, the problem may appear to be largely one affecting the elderly; on another, it may appear as a problem of large families. Policy priorities may be changed by the adoption of a different set of definitions.

In order to illustrate how appropriate choices of definition can affect the apparent seriousness of the problem,[3] I begin with a case study of comparing poverty in France and the United Kingdom,[4] on the basis of the European Commission definition of poverty as having an income below 50 per cent of the average in the country in question. At first sight, this is a tight specification of the poverty criterion – and one that may be considered by many readers as having closed too many open questions – but even this apparently well-defined criterion allows quite a lot of room for manoeuvre. To be decided are the definition of 'average', the choice of equivalence scale, and the weighting of households according to their size. Such matters may seem ones that can be relegated to footnotes, but in fact they can have an appreciable effect on the relative poverty measures in different countries.

We have also to consider the relation between the European Commission studies of poverty, cited in the Introduction, and *national studies* of poverty, that is studies from individual Member States. In most European countries there have been studies carried out by government statisticians, independent research institutions, or by academics. In France, estimates have been made by statisticians at the Institut National de la Statistique et des Études Économiques (INSEE). Assémat and Glaude (1989) make use of data from two sources: the income tax declarations, and the household budget survey. It is the latter, the Enquête sur les Budgets Familiaux, which has been used by the European Commission, and it is on this that I focus here. In Britain, the Department of Social Security (DSS) has carried out regular studies of Households Below Average Income (HBAI), which gives estimates of the percentage of households below different

---

3 For an analysis of three different studies for the United Kingdom, see Johnson and Webb (1991), who bring out the sensitivity of results to the choice of definition.
4 This case study was carried out jointly with Karen Gardiner, Valérie Lechene and Holly Sutherland. A fuller version is given in Atkinson, Gardiner, Lechene and Sutherland (1993).

percentages of average income (Department of Social Security, 1991, 1992, 1993, 1994, 1995 and 1996).[5] They were until 1994/5 based on the same source, the Family Expenditure Survey, as the estimates by the European Commission.[6] It is natural to ask how the numbers presented by the European Commission correspond to the findings of these national studies. To the extent that they are different, how can the differences be explained?

The Commission's estimates quoted in the Introduction (table 0.1) show in the late 1980s there were 8.2 million poor people in France, 14.7 per cent of the total population, and 8.4 million in the United Kingdom, or 14.8 per cent of the population. The poverty rate in the later 1980s was, on this basis, virtually the same in the United Kingdom as in France. (Hagenaars et al. (1994, table 3.4) show the purchasing power of the poverty line as being essentially the same in the two countries.) As noted in the Introduction, the European Community estimates relate to the *household* population, excluding those living in institutions and the homeless, and the re- sults for the late 1980s take expenditure, rather than income, as the indicator of resources. With regard to the first of these points, the Commission's estimates follow the same practice as in the national studies of poverty considered here, which cover only those living in households. The national studies do, however, differ in that they take *income* as the indicator of resources. The significance of this difference is discussed in section 1.3 below; here, I take income as the indicator, so that we should not expect the results to mirror exactly those in table 0.1.

In this case study, we start from the approach adopted in the national study for France by Assémat and Glaude, applying this to the household budget survey data for the two countries for 1985 (the most recent available when we carried out the study,

5 The HBAI estimates have recently been criticized by Pryke in forceful terms: he describes them as 'economic nonsense' (1995, p. 70). A number of points correspond to those made here, but I take them as indicative of the sensitivity of the estimates to the assumptions made, rather than as a reason for ceasing to publish them.

The geographical coverage of the HBAI studies has varied over time. The first sets of estimates covered Great Britain (i.e. England, Wales and Scot- land, but not Northern Ireland); the subsequent estimates covered the United Kingdom (i.e. including Northern Ireland). The term 'Britain' is used on occasion in the text to cover both when the precise geographical coverage is not crucial.

6 From 1994/5, the estimates are based on the Family Resources Survey (FRS), which has a larger sample size and contains more detailed questions on benefit income. The FRS is limited to Great Britain and does not collect information about expenditure. See Department of Social Security (1996).

Table 1.1 Estimated size of low-income population on different definitions: France 1984/5 and the United Kingdom 1985

Definition	France — Proportion less than 40%	50%	60%	United Kingdom — Proportion less than 40%	50%	60%
A: median households OECD scale before housing	5.3	9.6	16.8	1.7	4.1	9.9
median		48,937 FF per year			£70.44 a week	
B: *mean* households OECD scale before housing	7.0	13.5	22.5	3.1	9.2	20.9
mean		54,604 FF per year			£83.09 a week	
C: mean *individuals* OECD scale before housing	6.4	12.5	22.0	3.8	10.3	21.0
mean		51,356 FF per year			£80.01 a week	
D: mean individuals *DSS scale* before housing	6.5	11.9	20.1	2.6	8.6	19.9
mean		57,188 FF per year			£86.58 a week	
E: mean individuals DSS scale *after housing*	7.4	13.0	21.2	5.3	13.6	25.0
mean		44,739 FF per year			£67.13 a week	

and a further reason why the results may differ from those in table 0.1). We begin with line A in table 1.1.[7] There are on this basis about 10 per cent of the French population in poverty, a figure which may be contrasted with the much smaller proportion – around 4 per cent – in the United Kingdom when measured in this way.

The Assémat and Glaude definition is, however, a different interpretation of '50 per cent of the average' from that adopted in the UK study by the Department of Social Security (DSS). We now examine the effect of moving step by step to the United Kingdom definition. There are four main ingredients:

Choice of mean or median

The simplest difference is that the French take the median as the measure of the average, whereas the DSS study in the United Kingdom, and the EC in their work, take the mean. The choice between these is in part a matter of their relative statistical properties.[8] The choice is however also a question of the *level* of the poverty line. As may be seen from table 1.1, the median is 85 per cent of the mean in the United Kingdom and 90 per cent in France. Taking 50 per cent of the median is like taking a cut-off of 45 per cent or 42.5 per cent of the mean. The figures are therefore higher with 50 per cent of the mean, and they are higher to a different extent in the two countries. Poverty in the United Kingdom is now around half as much again in France, rather than twice as much.

Weighting of different units

The second difference concerns the weights to be applied to each individual household. As noted by O'Higgins and Jenkins (1990), the mean or median can be calculated in different ways depending on how the units are weighted, and the same applies to the calculation of the proportion with low incomes. For each household we calculate

7 The 9.6 per cent figure in table 1.1 corresponds to that of 10.1 per cent figure in the Assémat and Glaude study. The difference shows that we have not succeeded in fully in reproducing their calculations; nonetheless it is sufficiently close for our purposes.

8 It may be argued that the median is less subject to sampling fluctuations (on certain assumptions about the form of the income distribution). We should also note that, while the median is unaffected by the top or bottom coding of observations, it is affected by the deletion of observations, such as those with zero incomes.

the income per equivalent adult. (We discuss the equivalence scales below.) If the total income of household h is y_h, and the number of equivalent adults e_h, then the equivalent income is y_h/e_h, and it is according to this that the households are ranked. The question is now – how do we weight these households when adding them up? There are at least three possibilities (Atkinson and Cazes, 1990): a weight of unity to each household, a weight of e_h to household h, and a weight equal to the number of individuals in household h. The first of these methods has been applied in French studies; the third is that applied in the DSS study in the United Kingdom.

It might not appear to be a question of much importance. However, it may be seen from a comparison of lines B and C in table 1.1 that the difference between the estimates for each country individually is fairly small – of the order of 1 per centage point – but that they move the two countries in opposite directions. The poverty count is reduced in France and increased in the United Kingdom, so that is now only around a quarter higher in France.

Choice of equivalence scale

Third there is the choice of equivalence scale. The equivalence scale applied in the analysis of the French EBF by Assémat and Glaude (1989) is simple: 1 for the first adult, 0.7 for other adults and 0.5 for children aged less than 14. This scale is that typically referred to as 'the OECD scale' (see OECD, 1982), and I adopt the same shorthand here, even if it has no official status. This scale tends to be relatively generous to large families, and for this reason Hagenaars et al. in the results of table 0.1 (in the Introduction) use a 'modified OECD scale' with 0.5 for additional adults and 0.3 for children aged 14 or younger (1994, p 18). In contrast to the relatively simple OECD scale, that applied in the DSS study in the United Kingdom varies the amount per additional adult according to the number in the household (and is less for the spouse of the household head) and the amount per child is graded with age.

The effect of adopting the DSS scale in both countries is shown in line D of table 1.1.[9] This goes in the opposite direction to the previ-

9 The 8.6 per cent figure for the United Kingdom may be compared with the 9.2 per cent estimate of the DSS (1988b, table C1). There are, however, several reasons why the figure may differ, apart from our failure to reproduce exactly their calculations. Among these are the fact that we include Northern Ireland (the DSS estimates for 1985 related to Great Britain), and that we have tried to align the definition of income with that in the French data, including certain lump-sum payments such as that for redundancy.

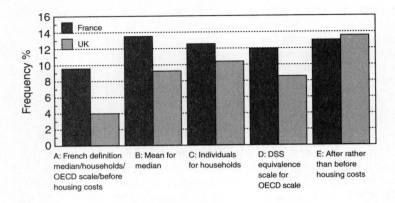

Figure 1.1 Different interpretations of EC standard: France and United Kingdom compared 1985. Percentage below 50 per cent income.
Source: Atkinson et al. (1993).

ous change, reducing both poverty counts and widening the gap again, so that poverty in France is now 40 per cent higher than in the United Kingdom.

Before or after housing costs

The calculations carried out by the DSS in Britain are made on two bases: before and after housing costs. In the former case, the figures relate to the distribution of equivalent net income, which includes housing benefit but makes no deduction for housing costs (including the interest paid on loans for house purchase). In the latter case, what is measured is net resources, defined as net income minus housing expenditure, again expressed per equivalent adult.

The second of these calculations – that of net resources after housing costs – may appear rather strange to observers from outside the United Kingdom. It can, however, be justified on the grounds that housing expenditure is a relatively exogenous element of a household's outgoings and one which varies across households in a way which reflects accidents of geographical location and tenure rather than the quality of the accommodation occupied. Such a view does not necessarily mean that we should concentrate *solely* on net resources, but a case can be made for considering its implications. These are shown in line E in table 1.1. In France the difference is small, but in the United Kingdom it is large, and the poverty percentage is now higher than that in France. The difference between the countries is probably not statistically significant, but the picture is certainly different from that where we began.

Conclusion

The different findings with regard to the proportion of the population below 50 per cent of average income are summarized in figure 1.1, which demonstrates that the choice of definition can make a noticeable difference to the results. If we imagine the politicians as having agreed on a 50 per cent of average target, and then left the details to their economists or statisticians, then the latter could come up with very different pictures depending how they interpreted the brief. Adopting a definition like that in the French study of Assémat and Glaude – with 50 per cent of the median, weighting households as 1, applying the OECD equivalence scale, and taking income before housing costs – we find poverty to be more than twice as high in France as in the United Kingdom. Adopting the definition used in the official British study, with 50 per cent of the mean, counting people not households, with the DSS equivalence scale, and taking income after housing costs, there seems to be little difference in the extent of poverty. A criterion of 50 per cent of average income, or expenditure, may appear at first sight unambiguous, but it leaves a number of matters to be decided.

A second cautionary tale: poverty trends in Ireland

A second example of the importance of definitions is provided by the recent trends in poverty in Ireland, as illustrated by the very interesting evidence of Callan et al. (1996). They use data from two surveys carried out by the Economic and Social Research Institute (ESRI) to investigate whether poverty in Ireland increased between 1987 and 1994. In the results cited here, poverty is defined as 50 per cent of mean disposable income per equivalent adult averaged over households.[10]

The answer depends on the definitions and measures adopted. A

10 As Callan et al. (1996, p. 66), note the procedure of averaging over *households* is different from that used by the DSS in the UK when constructing the HBAI estimates, where the average is taken over *individuals*. Applied to the Irish 1994 data, the latter method yields poverty figures which are about 2–3 percentage points lower (1996, p. 70).

Pessimist would be impressed by the set of estimates in diagram A of figure 1.2 which are labelled SWA and show a rise in poverty. In each case, I have normalized the findings so that 1987 = 100; in fact the proportion in poverty rose from 16.3 per cent to 18.5 per cent. An Optimist however may point out that this depends on using the equivalence scale approximating the Supplementary Welfare Allowance (hence the label SWA).[11] This scale gives relatively little weight to children (0.33 compared with a single adult), whereas the OECD scale gives a weight of 0.5. When Callan et al. apply the OECD scale to the Irish data, then the results are different: poverty appears to have fallen, as shown by the line labelled OECD in diagram A of figure 1.2.

The Pessimist now returns to the attack with diagram B in figure 1.2. Here he accepts the OECD scale, but takes the Optimist to task for counting households. After all, in a democratic society surely each person should count for 1? We should not give the same weight to a single person as to a couple with four children. This takes us from the line labelled 'Households' (which is the same as that labelled 'OECD' in diagram A) to that labelled 'Persons'. Poverty has increased.

The Optimist, however, while agreeing that the number of people in poverty has risen, goes on to argue that we should be concerned not just with counting the number of poor people but with how far they fall below the poverty line. If a family is £1 a month below the poverty line, this is less serious than if they are £50 below. This points to measuring the *poverty gap*, or the amount of money by which people fall below. From diagram C in figure 1.2, where the line labelled 'Headcount' is the same as that labelled 'Persons' in diagram B, it may be seen that use of the poverty gap reverses the conclusion drawn. The poverty gap has fallen: serious poverty is less than it was.

This dialogue shows that there are no simple answers.

1.2 Absolute and Relative Standards

In the next three sections, I examine these definitional issues in greater depth, with particular reference to the two uses which have been illustrated in section 1.1: the comparison of poverty in different European countries, and the measurement of trends over time. I begin with the choice between 'absolute' and 'relative' standards. An absolute poverty line is usually taken to be one which is fixed over time in

11 The Supplementary Welfare Allowance is the safety-net social welfare scheme for those not eligible for other programmes.

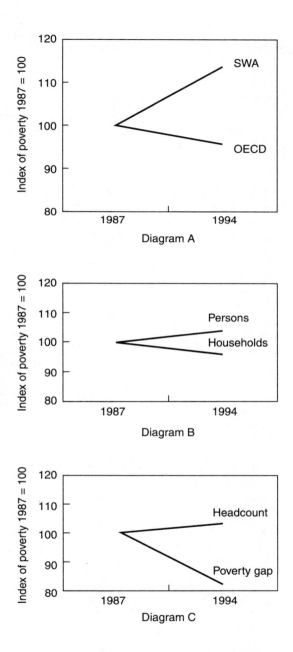

Figure 1.2   Change in poverty in Ireland.
Source: Callan et al. (1996), tables 4.9 and 4.10.

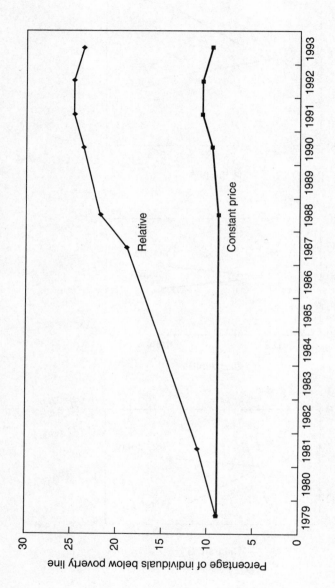

Figure 1.3 Constant purchasing power and relative poverty lines: UK 1979–1993/4.

Source: Department of Social Security (1992), (1993), (1995) and (1996), tables E1(AHC) and F1(AHC).

terms of purchasing power, allowing the purchase of a specified basket of goods and services which has some justification as the minimum 'necessary' or as representing 'basic needs'. A relative poverty line varies with changes in average incomes or expenditure, a simple example being a line which is fixed as a proportion of the average. The results for trends in poverty in Ireland just cited were based on a poverty standard which was 50 per cent of the mean income in the year in question. Since real incomes rose by about 17 per cent between 1987 and 1994, the poverty standard was appreciably higher in 1994 than if the 1987 standard had only been adjusted for the rise in consumer prices.

In the United Kingdom, the official HBAI estimates referred to in the previous section show the trends over time in terms both of a relative standard (50% of the current average income) and of a standard adjusted only for price changes (50% of the 1979 real average income). Since real incomes per head have increased substantially (40% between 1979 and 1993/4), this makes a big difference – see figure 1.3 (which shows the results where income is measured after housing costs). Both figures coincide for 1979 (the base year). Thereafter, on a relative basis poverty has increased very sharply over the period as a whole, whereas on a constant price basis, there has been little change. The official Italian estimates show that over a similar period (1980 to 1994), poverty rose slightly on a relative basis (from 8.3% to 10.2%) but fell sharply on a constant real income basis (to 3.4%) (Commissione di indagine sulla povertà et l'emarginazione, 1996, Tav. 3).

These show that different approaches may yield different results. They also draw our attention to the difference between a standard which simply holds the poverty line constant in terms of purchasing power, as in these examples, and one which has a justification in terms of its absolute level. No particular claim is made in the HBAI study that the 1979 level is an appropriate one (just as the choice of 50%, rather than some other per centage, has a degree of arbitrariness). We may distinguish therefore between a *constant real income standard* and an *absolute standard*, the latter being illustrated by the approaches adopted in a number of countries.

Methods adopted in different countries

In the United Kingdom, Seebohm Rowntree's pioneering study in York in 1899 was based on

the minimum necessaries for the maintenance of merely physical efficiency. (Rowntree, 1901, p. 117 in 1922 edition)

[21]

This is an example of the absolute approach: he defined people to be in poverty if they could not afford a specified basket of goods. More formally, the poverty line π is based on a vector x^* of goods, purchasable at prices p:

$$\pi = p \cdot x^* \tag{1.1}$$

In defining x^*, Rowntree drew on the research of early nutritionists to define the food components. He also made reference to the dietaries used to feed people in institutions. This was his justification for including tea in the list of goods. It has little or no nutritional value but its replacement in Bradford Workhouse by a more nutritive soup led to a riot.

In the United States, the official poverty line devised by Mollie Orshansky (1965) had similarities, starting from the US Department of Agriculture's 'economy food plan' for households of different composition, with non-food requirements being taken into account by multiplying by the reciprocal of an estimated food share (a factor of 3): i.e.

$$\pi = h \, p_f \cdot x^*_f \tag{1.2}$$

where x^*_f denotes food requirements, p_f denotes the vector of food prices, and h is the multiplier. The intention was to adjust the poverty line solely in relation to prices. Nonetheless, there have been pressures for periodic adjustments, even if at long intervals. Robert Lampman, for example, argued that the poverty line should be adjusted only for price changes, but that it should be

> a goal unique to this generation. That goal should be achieved before 1980, at which time the next generation will have set new economic and social goals. (1971, p. 53)

(We now know that this was over-optimistic. It takes much longer to revise the poverty goal, let alone abolish poverty, as is illustrated by the recent report proposing adjustments to the official poverty line – see Citro and Michael (1995).) There are also those in the United States who have argued for an explicitly relative poverty standard, such as Victor Fuchs (1965) who proposed that the poverty threshold should be set at one half of median income.

In the United Kingdom, Rowntree too was conscious of the problems involved in applying an absolute standard over long periods of time, and in his subsequent surveys in 1936 (Rowntree, 1941) and 1950 (Rowntree and Lavers, 1951), the real value of the scale was substantially higher than in 1899. The critique of Rowntree's work by Peter Townsend (1954 and 1962) made a powerful case for a relative standard. Townsend's study with Brian Abel-Smith, *The Poor and the Poorest* (1965), used the assistance benefit scale, a scale which had increased in real terms over time; and Townsend's major study of poverty (1979) developed the use of indicators of relative deprivation.

The implications of using administrative benefit scales as a poverty criterion depend on policy towards benefits. In practice, they have tended to increase in real terms but not necessarily by as much as average incomes. Gustafsson and Uusitalo (1990, p. 255) compare the rise for Finland in median income compared with the rise in the full national pension for an old person who has no other income (which they state to be close to the public assistance level). Between 1966 and 1985, median income in Finland doubled in real terms, whereas the national pension increased by 66 per cent. Hauser and Semrau (1989, diagram 1) compare the movement in the standard rate of social assistance in West Germany with those in prices and in the net wage per worker. From 1963 to 1969, the social assistance level increased broadly in line with prices, while wages rose in real terms, but there were then a series of upward adjustments and by the mid-1970s the social assistance scale had caught up with net wages. From that point, the social assistance scale increased somewhat less fast in real terms than wages.

A quite different approach is where the poverty standard is based on 'subjective' definitions of poverty, based on survey responses to questions about the adequacy of income in terms of some particular target (making ends meet, not being poor, having a very good income, etc.), as in the 'Leyden approach'.[12] When public opinion is asked about the minimum necessary income, the answers tend to produce a poverty line which rises in real terms. In the United States, for example, the Gallup Poll has regularly asked the question:

> What is the smallest amount of money a family of four needs each week to get along in this community?

And an analysis of the responses over the period 1957–71 by Kilpatrick (1973) showed that they tended to rise about 0.6 per cent for each 1 per cent rise in per capita income. On this basis, the poverty line would have increased in real terms by some 25 per cent between 1959 and 1971.

12 The approach was developed by Bernard van Praag and colleagues then working at Leyden University. See, for example, van Praag, Hagenaars and van Weeren (1982), and Goedhart et al. (1977), de Vos (1991), and de Vos and Garner (1991).

There are, therefore, several different approaches to the adjustment of the poverty standard over time: (a) an absolute standard, based on the cost of a bundle of basic goods and services, adjusted only for price changes, (b) a constant real income standard set historically and then adjusted only for price changes, (c) an absolute standard adjusted for price changes but with periodic (generational) adjustments as new goals are set, (d) a scale which rises regularly in real terms but by less than average incomes, and (e) thorough-going relativity, as with the EC standard of 50 per cent of average income.

Standard of living and minimum rights approaches

How can these different types of standard be justified? In thinking about this, and other, definitional questions, I find it helpful to contrast *a standard of living approach* and *a minimum rights approach*. The standard of living approach is typified by the Rowntree studies of York already described. This may be contrasted with the second approach which sees poverty in terms of deprivation of a certain minimum right to resources. People are seen as entitled to a minimum income, which is a prerequisite for participation in a particular society. It may be linked to citizenship, in that a certain minimum level of resources is necessary in order that people may enjoy effective freedom.

The distinction between the standard of living and minimum rights conceptions helps clarify thinking about the definitional problems, even if in practice the two notions are often confounded. Applied to the distinction between absolute and relative conceptions of poverty, it allows us to identify the different arguments which can be made. On a minimum rights approach, this is explicitly a matter for judgement. A case could be made for an essential minimum which is fixed in absolute terms or for one which is expressed as a proportion of an average for the society in which those rights are guaranteed. If average incomes rise, as the society becomes more prosperous, then, on the latter basis, the poverty line would rise in real terms. If average incomes fall, for example as a result of increased unemployment, then the poverty line would fall. (This may indicate a need to smooth the changes over time.) One argument pointing to a relative version of the minimum rights criterion is that of transparency. John Rawls, in his theory of justice (1971), stressed the importance of the public nature of principles and their verifiability. A poverty standard of 50 per cent of the average, while not unambiguous, as we have seen, is readily explained, at least in principle. This may mean that there is greater confidence that it can be verified.

[24]

The position with the standard of living approach is at first sight clearcut. Consideration of basic needs leads to the vector x^* in equation (1.1), and the poverty line should be adjusted over time on account of price rises.[13] As average incomes rise, so the poverty line will fall behind. If there are short-run fluctuations in average income, then they will not be reflected in the poverty line. There are however evident difficulties with this approach, if it is applied over long intervals, and this may be the reason why periodic adjustments have been proposed.

First, if we maintain unchanged the list of goods, x^*, then over time a number of these goods will cease to be readily *available*. As living standards in general improve, shops stop selling certain types of good, such as cheaper cuts of meat; increasingly, one cannot buy goods in small quantities or without expensive packaging (for instance, it is not easy today to buy butter loose). Second, the goods in the list x^* may not have the same significance today. When describing his allowance for clothing in 1899, Rowntree said that it

> should not be so shabby as to injure his chances of obtaining respectable employment. (1922, p. 140)

But in order to apply for a job today, a person needs a different standard of dress from that expected in 1899. New goods come into existence, displacing other – possibly cheaper – goods, but they may be necessary to perform the same function. If other job seekers have a telephone, then people without one cannot compete on equal terms: they risk 'social exclusion'. Goods are a means to carrying out certain activities. We cannot ignore what is happening around us when assessing poverty, even on an absolute basis. This social exclusion aspect is developed further in the second Lecture. Third, there may be changes in social roles. Rowntree's reference to *his* chances of obtaining employment highlights the way in which the role of women is now very different from that at the beginning of the century. The high proportion of women in the paid labour market has to be reflected in the list of necessary goods, including, for example, the addition of child-care costs. A fixed bundle of goods and services does not seem a defensible basis for a poverty line in Europe.

An alternative way of thinking about this issue is the *capabilities* approach advocated by Amartya Sen. He has made a forceful case that assessment of the standard of living should focus on a person's

---

13 There is an important issue, not discussed here, of the choice of price index where relative prices change. See Muellbauer (1974) for an extensive treatment of this issue.

capabilities (Sen, 1983, 1985 and 1992).[14] He illustrates this by the example of a bicycle:

> It is, of course, a commodity. It has several characteristics, and let us concentrate on one particular characteristic, viz., transportation. Having a bike gives a person the ability to move about in a certain way that he may not be able to do without the bike. So the transportation *characteristic* of the bike gives the person the *capability* of moving in a certain way. That capability may give the person utility. (1983, p. 160)

Sen argues that, in this chain

Commodities → Characteristics → Capability → Utility

it is

> 'the third category – that of capability to function – that comes closest to the notion of standard of living'. (1983, p. 160)

For Sen, the capabilities approach provides a basis for

> sorting out . . . the absolute-relative disputation in the conceptualization of poverty. At the risk of oversimplification, I would like to say that poverty is an absolute notion in the space of capabilities but very often it will take a relative form in the space of commodities or characteristics. (1983, p. 161)

The goods required to achieve a specified set of capabilities can be expected to change over time:

> In a country that is generally rich, more income may be needed to buy enough commodities to achieve the *same social functioning*, such as 'appearing in public without shame'. The same applies to the capability of 'taking part in the life of the community. (Sen, 1992, p. 115)

A poverty line fixed in real terms does not take this into account.

Conclusions

The main conclusion that I draw is that, in comparisons over time, a fixed bundle of goods is unlikely to prove an acceptable basis for a

14 For further discussion of Sen's ideas, see, among others, Anand and Ravallion (1993), Sugden (1993), Balestrino (1994), Herrero (1995), Martinetti (1996), and Stewart (1996); for studies implementing the capability or functionings approach, see Schokkaert and Van Ootegem (1990), Lovell et al. (1990), and Balestrino (1996).

long-run poverty measure in Europe. Even on a standard of living approach, there need to be increases in the real value to allow for the non-availability of goods and for changes in their significance. An absolute standard must contain provisions for periodic revision. This is reinforced if we consider the concept of social exclusion, interpreted to mean people being prevented from participation in the normal activities of the society in which they live or being incapable of functioning. Even if the level of activities, or capabilities, is taken as fixed, this may well require a rising real volume of goods and services. It does not follow that the poverty line should be expressed as a proportion of average income, but there are arguments along minimum rights lines which would support such a conclusion: a standard of 50 per cent of the average has the virtues of simplicity and transparency.

A Europe-wide standard?

Comparisons across countries raise issues which are different, but related. They did not arise at all seriously in the case study of France and the United Kingdom, since we were considering two countries with relatively similar levels of average (mean) income or expenditure per head. If, however, we widen the comparison to include countries such as Greece or Portugal, then we have to consider the implications of different income levels across countries.

Rather than applying a poverty standard based on the average expenditure in each Member State, as in table 0.1 in the Introduction, we could apply the same standard, adjusted for purchasing power differences, in all countries.[15] This would lead to higher poverty figures being recorded in countries where the average expenditure is below the EU average, and reduced figures those in the countries where average expenditure is above the EU average. The implications of moving to such a Community-wide poverty line, rather than using national lines, is shown in figure 1.4, based on the estimates of de Vos and Zaidi (1996). As may be seen, there are major changes in the composition of the poverty population. With country-specific poverty lines, Spain (E), Greece and Portugal account for 18 per cent of the poor in Europe; with a Community-wide poverty line, the proportion rises to 29 per cent. It remains the case, however, that a sizeable fraction of the poor in Europe are in rich countries: a quarter are in France and West Germany.

Can our earlier analysis cast light on this choice? On a minimum

15 Alternatively, we could apply the poverty line of country i to country j, as in van Praag et al. (1982).

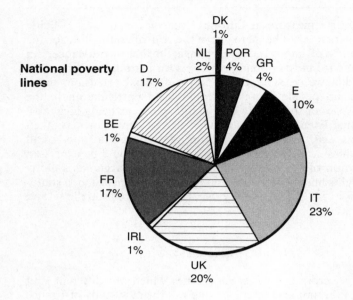

National poverty lines

DK 1%
NL 2%
POR 4%
GR 4%
D 17%
E 10%
BE 1%
FR 17%
IT 23%
IRL 1%
UK 20%

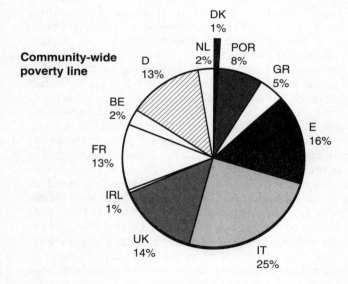

Community-wide poverty line

DK 1%
NL 2%
POR 8%
D 13%
GR 5%
BE 2%
E 16%
FR 13%
IRL 1%
UK 14%
IT 25%

Figure 1.4 National versus Community-wide estimates of poverty in the late 1980s. *Source:* de Vos and Zaidi (1996), table 1.

rights approach, it is a political judgement whether we apply a relative poverty line *within* each Member State (as in table 0.1), or whether we consider that people have rights as Europeans. In the latter case, which represents a significant move towards viewing the European Union as a social entity, we would apply a poverty standard based on the average for the Union as a whole, as in the lower part of figure 1.4.

On a standard of living approach, use of the same poverty standard in terms of purchasing power in each Member State has an obvious rationale. Allowance has of course to be made for differences between countries in the vector x^*: for example, differences in heating costs (the same may apply within Member States). Moreover, as we have seen, the standard may need to be modified if there are differences in the availability of goods, or if goods have different significance in social functioning. For instance, the requirements for job seekers may be different in a rich European country from those in a less rich country.

These considerations may point to a poverty line which lies between a fully national and an EU-wide one. In Atkinson (1990), I proposed use of an intermediate poverty line, where a parameter ι governs the relative weights on the European Union average (Y_{EU}) and the average for country i (Y_i):

$$50\% \text{ of } Y_{EU}{}^{\theta} Y_i^{(1-\theta)} \tag{1.3}$$

For example, θ equal to a half means that the poverty line applied in country i would be 50 per cent of the geometric mean of its own national average income and the European Union average. As has been suggested to me by Andrea Brandolini, how close θ is to 1 could be taken as an indicator of the degree of European convergence.

The proposal of a weighted average of national and EU poverty lines illustrates one general approach to the issues of definition, which is to devise ways in which a range of results can be presented in an intelligible manner, allowing for a range of different judgments. If, for example, a conclusion holds for all values of θ in the relevant range, then we can reach a conclusion without requiring full agreement about the balance between national and EU standards. This general approach will be used again in later sections.

1.3 Expenditure versus Income, Households versus Families, and Choice of Equivalence Scale

Family A has an income of only 45 per cent of the average, but maintains its spending at 55 per cent of the average by running down its savings. Should they be considered to be in poverty according to the EC 50 per cent standard? Their neighbours, Family B, have an income of 50 per cent of the average but spend only 45 per cent. Are they poor? Why should a single man spending x Euros be considered to be in poverty when a couple and a child with an income of less than $2x$ Euros are deemed to be above the poverty line? A couple and three children have a poverty level income, but their grown-up son lives with them, and his income takes them above the poverty line. Are they no longer poor? How do we resolve these definitional questions: (a) the choice between income and expenditure as an indicator of resources, (b) the choice between the household as a unit of analysis and a smaller unit such as the nuclear family, and (c) the implications of different assumptions about equivalence scales? While the last of these questions has been much discussed, the income/expenditure choice and the definition of the unit of analysis have been less fully examined. In what follows, I examine each of the three issues in turn, although it has to be remembered that they are inter-related. If, for example, we are concerned about expenditure, then it may not be possible to consider a smaller unit than the household, since some elements of household expenditure cannot be allocated to sub-units.

These definitional questions are related to the selection of data sources, since the information collected varies from one source to another. All European Union countries have a household budget survey, in which information is collected about household expenditure: for example, the Enquête sur les Budgets des Ménages in Belgium, the Enquête sur les Budgets Familiaux in France, the Household Budget Survey in Ireland, the Indagine sui Consumi delle Famiglie in Italy, and the Family Expenditure Survey in the United Kingdom. The budget surveys typically also contain income information, although the extent of detail and quality differs. But there are also other sources, such as the Bank of Italy survey or the ESRI Survey in Ireland, which contain income but not expenditure information. There are studies based on administrative records, such as those from income tax returns (in France, the Enquête sur les Revenus Fiscaux), which again cover income but not expenditure. These sources differ also in the extent to which they allow disaggregation of the household unit.

One important respect in which data sources differ is the extent to which they provide information which can be used to supplement that on income or expenditure as measures of economic poverty. Reference should be made to the study of indicators of deprivation pioneered in Britain by Townsend (1979) and Mack and Lansley (1985), developed by Desai and Shah (1988). In this case, poverty is defined in terms of the lack of perceived necessities, with particular reference to enforced lack (rather than chosen life-styles). In Ireland, the relation between income poverty and deprivation indicators is explored by Callan et al. (1993, 1996), and Nolan and Whelan (1996 and 1996a).[16] Reference should equally be made to the examination of the non-cash benefits from government expenditure (see Smeeding et al., 1993 and Gardiner et al., 1995). In what follows, attention is concentrated on income and expenditure, but these are only part of the picture.

Expenditure versus income

In Italy, the estimates of poverty made by the official Commissione di indagine sulla povertà of poverty are based on the expenditure of households; in Sweden official estimates are based on household income. In the United Kingdom there has been a shift from the use of expenditure, as in pre-war studies of poverty, to income as the indicator of resources (for example, in the official Households Below Average Income (HBAI) studies). The European Commission, on the other hand, has made the reverse switch,[17] from using income in its earlier studies to using expenditure in the findings for the late 1980s quoted in table 0.1. (And the latest Eurostat (1997) estimates revert to household income.) How can these choices be justified?

Discussion of the choice between income and expenditure is confounded by the fact that there are several different sets of considerations. First, we need to distinguish between the question as to *what we want to measure* and the issue as to how far *we can measure* what we want to measure. The latter, is of great importance, and influences much practice. The European Commission, for example, appear to believe that *in principle* income should be the indicator; their adoption of expenditure is on practical grounds. They argue that expenditure is a more reliable indicator of 'true' income than income reported in budget surveys, although how far this is true varies from country to country (and it has to be remembered that there are alternative sources to the budget surveys). Hagenaars et al. conclude that:

16 For Finland, see Kangas and Ritakallio (1995); for France, see Lollivier and Verger (1997); for Sweden, see Halleröd (1995); for Australia, see Travers (1996) and Saunders (1997).
17 Rather confusingly, when the switch was first made the Commission report continued to refer to 'income', with only a footnote to alert the reader to the fact that 'expenditure . . . has been used throughout as an approximation of average per capita income' (European Commission, 1991, p. 2).

> The main argument in favour of using expen-ditures instead of income
> as an indicator for resources relates to the quality of the data. Mainly
> due to the fact that in the Household Budget Surveys the focus is on
> expenditures . . . the accuracy of the reported incomes is rather doubt-
> ful in a number of Member States. (1994, p. 6)

There is undoubtedly under-reporting of income, particularly of certain types, although they recognise that expenditure too poses problems of under-reporting.[18]

Turning to issues of principle, we may find an answer in the distinction drawn earlier between standard of living and minimum rights
approaches. On a standard of living approach, it may appear self-
evident that consumption should be the variable studied. We are
concerned with whether people actually have access to a specified
basket of goods and services (indeed we may be concerned with particular items, such as housing or food). On this basis, Family A with
spending at 55 per cent of the average is above the poverty line. On
a minimum rights basis, however, people are entitled to a minimum
income, the disposal of which is a matter for them. Family A is
below the poverty line, because its income is only 45 per cent of the
average.

Such a clear-cut answer is, however, blurred by a second set of
considerations: those involving time. People's incomes and spending
diverge over the life-cycle for well-known reasons. In part, this is
taken into account in the equivalence scales which adjust for differences in family size, but these do not typically allow for retirement.
In general people save, either independently or via state or occupational pension schemes, for their retirement, so that when they dissave
in old age we observe consumption in excess of income. Since people
may be expected to take into consideration, when making their consumption decisions, the capital market opportunities open to them
and their expectations regarding the future, this provides the standard argument in favour of looking at poverty in terms of consumption. Nonetheless, as noted by Blundell and Preston (1995), this may
lead to problems when comparing people born at different dates who
face different rates of real return, since faced with the same lifetime
flows of income they may make different consumption decisions. The
same applies to people in the same cohort who face different rates of
return. People with profitable investment opportunities may consume

---

18 McGregor and Borooah (1992) have analysed the income and expenditure data from the 1985 Family Expenditure Survey in the United Kingdom,
combined with the information on durable ownership. They argue that more
confidence can be placed in the expenditure measure, although this refers to
a standard of living approach to measuring poverty.

less today, and we cannot read the same lesson from their low consumption.

The time dimension encompasses not only longer-term life-cycle variation but also short-term fluctuations. Income can vary from month to month, and families may be able to smooth out such variations holding expenditure stable. Family A may be expecting its income to return to 55 per cent of the average, and hence it may be wrong to classify them as deprived on account of a temporary fall in income. As with the life-cycle, by taking expenditure, rather than income, as our indicator, we are allowing families to form their own judgments about future prospects and about their capacity to borrow on the capital market. On the other hand, they may be spending on an unsustainable basis, and the low current income may be a warning of future financial problems. Moreover, we have to distinguish between *expenditure* and *consumption*. The distinction is evident in the case of durables. Family B in the example given earlier may save 10 per cent of their income regularly to replace their durables; their consumption may be 50 per cent of the average, so that they are (just) not poor. Adjustments have been made to estimate the flow of consumption services (see, for example, Slesnick, 1993). But, as has been argued by Kay, Keen and Morris (1984), much expenditure has a durable element: clothes, leisure goods, stocks of household goods, and even the memory of a good dinner. As a result,

> observed expenditures are liable to give a seriously distorted picture of the true incidence of poverty [as indicated by consumption]. (Kay, Keen and Morris, 1984, p. 170)

We are brought back to the practical problems.

Finally, it may appear that the minimum rights approach avoids the issues of timing. It can simply be stated as a matter of principle that a person is entitled to a minimum inflow of resources. However, it is not evident that we would want to ignore the level of assets over which a person has control. If that is the case, then we face the problem of combining income and assets.

In view of the problems outlined above, there are good reasons for considering a range of approaches and examining the sensitivity of the findings. For the United Kingdom, Goodman, Johnson and Webb (1997) (see also Goodman and Webb, 1995 and 1995a) show that in 1992/3 the proportion below 50 per cent of the mean was 20.1 per cent on the basis of income and 18.6 per cent on the basis of expenditure. These are close, and the distribution of household expenditure shows a rise in poverty over time, like that in the household income distribution, but it differs in the extent and timing. On the other

[33]

hand, the composition of the group in poverty is different – see Goodman and Webb (1995).

Households versus families

In the United Kingdom, there has been a shift in official statistics from the family unit to the household as the unit of analysis. Whereas the earlier Low Income Families (LIF) statistics were based on an inner family unit,[19] the Households Below Average Income (HBAI) series which replaced them is based on the more extensive unit of people 'living at the same address having meals prepared together and with common housekeeping'. Among the arguments for this change were that most people in such units are closely related, so that the household is close to the family unit as defined above, and that the living standards of its members are more likely to be related to the total income than to their individual income.

The switch to a household unit means that the resources of the household are aggregated, and compared with the poverty line for the household as a whole, even if there are in fact separate spending units or families which constitute the household. Suppose for instance that Mr and Mrs X's household includes their daughter aged 13, their unemployed son aged 20, a friend of the son who is living with the family, and a lodger (see figure 1.5). In the HBAI statistics their income is added up, and divided by the equivalence scale for five adults and one child; in the LIF statistics they would have counted as four units: one family (Mr and Mrs X and daughter), and three separate individual units.

The choice between household and family unit can make quite a difference. The effects of the change in definition in the United Kingdom on the results for 1983 have been investigated by Johnson and Webb (1989), who show that the proportion of the population with income below 50 per cent of the average is

    11.1 per cent on an inner family basis
    8.1 per cent on a household basis

In other words, there is a reduction of a quarter in the number of people with low incomes on switching to a household basis. This reflected a more general reduction in income inequality: the Gini coefficient for the household distribution is 26.1 per cent, compared

---

19 For discussion of the LIF series, see, among others, Atkinson (1983, ch. 10), Townsend (1990), and Johnson and Webb (1991).

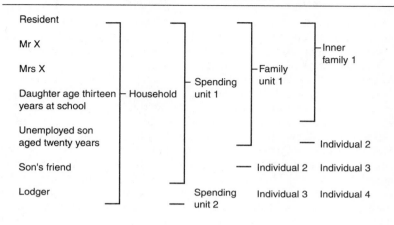

Figure 1.5 Different units of analysis: illustration.

with 28.5 per cent for the family distribution. Moreover the composition of the low-income population is changed in the direction of there being fewer single people without children and below pension age: the proportion of this group below half the national average falls to 8 per cent on a household basis, compared with 21 per cent on a family basis (Johnson and Webb, 1989, table 2).

A range of different definitions of the unit of analysis are possible, making use of elements such as the following:

(1) Common residence, with a *household* comprising those resident in a dwelling and sharing some degree of common house-keeping, the most extensive unit of analysis;
(2) Common spending, where the *spending unit* is defined as those taking spending decisions to a considerable degree in common, where this may cover people who have no family relationship;
(3) Blood or marital relationship, where members of the *family unit* are related by marriage/cohabitation or by blood relations; and
(4) Dependence, where the unit is defined to include a single person or couple plus any dependant children, this constituting the *inner family*.

The different possibilities are illustrated in figure 1.5. As set out there, the criteria are applied cumulatively, so that the family unit refers to those members of the family *resident in the same household*.

In considering the choice between different units, it is helpful to consider first the standard of living approach. There are items of consumption that are essentially individualistic, such as food, whereas there are other items that have some of the attributes of 'public goods' as far as individuals in the household are concerned, such as housing. In these latter cases, the spillover may be such that all members of the household enjoy broadly equal levels of living, but in the former case there may be considerable within-household inequality or gender inequality. The distribution of benefits within the unit is difficult to observe. It is therefore understandable that, for practical reasons, studies of poverty have often taken the household or spending unit, assuming that everyone within the unit shares the same standard of living. There are, however, good reasons in principle why we should be concerned about standards of living at the individual level. A couple may live together but nonetheless enjoy different standards of living. The standard of living of grown-up children living at home may be different from that of their parents. While most of the evidence relates to the household (as with the HBAI studies in the United Kingdom), we should be aware of the way in which this may mis-represent the extent and nature of individual poverty where resources are not in fact shared in the assumed manner.[20] It is only by looking within the household that issues such as the feminization of poverty can be adequately discussed.

On a rights approach, the theoretical concept of rights is usually assumed to be individualistic, but again there are practical problems arising from the fact that there are within-family transfers which cannot be adequately observed. It would be possible to measure poverty on an individual basis using information on the original source of income (see, for example, Sutherland, 1996). To each person would be attributed their earnings, benefit income, and their investment income (including a share of the income from joint assets). But it would not be satisfactory to ignore transfers within the family; we would not accept that a large number of those with zero recorded cash income are in fact without resources. It may therefore be necessary to assume that incomes are pooled, although this again ignores within-family inequality.

Transfers within the family raise the question of 'dependency'. A number of social commentators have argued that we should try to reduce dependency on the state, with a Euro of income from social security being valued less than a Euro that a person earns from his or her own efforts. But dependency is not simply a matter of state

---

20 See Jenkins (1991) for discussion of these issues. The empirical importance of intra-household inequality in a developing country has been investigated by Haddad and Kanbur (1990).

benefits and has to be viewed more broadly. Indeed, historically, one important role of state benefits has been to reduce dependency on the family, which also has negative aspects. As it has been put by Robert Goodin:

> depending upon their families for assistance subjects beneficiaries to the 'arbitrary will of another'. (Goodin, 1988, p. 351)

This has particular relevance to the treatment of couples. It may be quite wrong to treat all married couples as having equal rights to the joint income. Even if within-family transfers are such that total family income is equally divided, one cannot treat all sources of income as equivalent: 1,000 Euro earned by the wife may be valued more highly than 1,000 Euro given by her husband to pay for the housekeeping. Within the household, transfers from children to elderly parents may be conditional (for example on the old person going to live with the children) and may induce dependence. On a rights approach, there is a case for attempting to apply a 'discount' factor to transfers, both within the family and from the state.

Equivalence scales

In the second case study of Section 1.1, whether poverty in Ireland rose or fell depended on the choice of equivalence scale. The choice is therefore important. In the first case study, the change in equivalence scales from the OECD to DSS scale affected not just the level of poverty but also the relative poverty rates in France and the United Kingdom. This is not perhaps surprising in view of what we know about the differences in policy towards families of different sizes in the two countries. People tend to think in terms of French policy being more generous to families, whether in the form of income tax allowances (the quotient familial) or child benefits. In particular, the French child benefit system is more tilted in the direction of larger families.

The allowance to be made for households of different size is a matter about which people may legitimately disagree. In the empirical literature, we certainly find disagreement. A wide range of methods of calculating such scales has been employed, including the analysis of observed consumption behaviour, expert judgements about nutritional and other requirements, deriving the revealed preferences of governments in setting benefit levels or tax allowances, and questionnaire studies of people's views as to the adequacy of different incomes. They have led to very different results. The survey by Whiteford (1985, table 5.1) tabulates 44 estimates of the scale for a single person, taking that for a couple as 100 per cent, and these estimates vary from 49 per cent to 94 per cent. For a couple with two children, the same survey shows 59 estimates ranging from 111 per cent to 193 per cent. The geometric mean of the latter estimates is 138 per cent, but the OECD, for example, uses a figure of 159 per cent.

How can we allow for such differences of judgment? One useful approach is that suggested by Buhmann et al. (1988), who parameterize the equivalence scales as n^s. The exponent s is a valuable method of summarizing differences in scales. Buhmann et al. show that the scales used in statistical studies (such as the OECD scale) have an elasticity around 0.72. Scales based on benefit parameters tend to have values of s around 0.55; estimates based on observed consumption patterns and identifying restrictions tend to be lower (Buhmann et al. take a value of 0.36 as representative); scales based on subjective evaluations (of what is needed 'to get along') tend to be lower still (around 0.25). At the same time, the para-meterization is only very approximate and does not capture the variation by age or other characteristics that one finds within a household of a specified size.[21] Even the simple OECD scale, for example, for a household of five people ranges from 3.0 to 3.8, which would mean s varying from 0.68 to 0.83. The DSS scale used in the United Kingdom could in principle range from 1.89 (assuming a single parent with children aged 0, 1, 2 and 3) to 3.62, which would mean s varying from 0.4 to 0.8.

Figure 1.6 shows how the poverty measures for France and the United Kingdom vary with s, taking the equivalence scale as given by n^s. These estimates are otherwise the same as in lines C and D in table 1.1. In both cases, there is a U-shape, as has been examined in depth in work by Coulter et al. (1992). The trough in France appears to be around 0.55, that in the United Kingdom rather higher, around 0.65. It is the difference between the countries which is of particular interest here. The two curves intersect at a value of s around 0.55, with poverty higher in the United Kingdom if we take values below this. If one were to take a value of 0.25, as with the scales based on subjective evaluation, then the United Kingdom would have a poverty rate of 15.4 per cent compared with 13.0 per cent in France. On a per capita basis, the poverty rate in France is 16.5 per cent compared with 14.3 per cent in the United Kingdom.

It is not just the total in poverty which is affected but also the *composition*. Figure 1.7 shows the breakdown in France by size of household. With $s = 0$, households of 1 and 2 persons account for two-thirds of the total; with $s = 1$, those with 5 or more people

21 For discussion of versions with two or more parameters, see Cutler and Katz (1992), Banks and Johnson (1994), Jenkins and Cowell (1994), and Duclos and Mercader-Prats (1994).

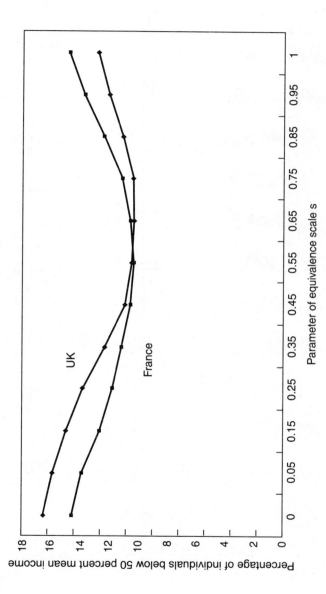

Figure 1.6 Sensitivity of poverty count to equivalence scale: France and United Kingdom 1985.
Source: Atkinson et al. (1993).

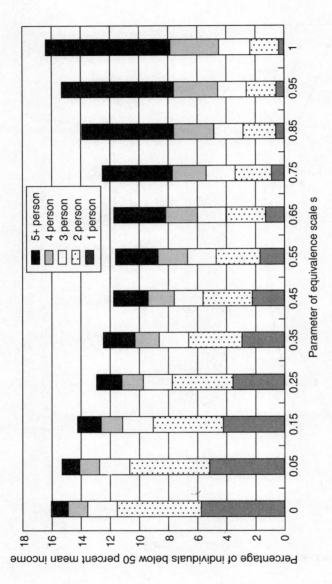

Figure 1.7 Composition of poor with different equivalence scales: France 1985.
Source: Atkinson et al. (1993), figure 5A.

account for a half. One gets a quite different picture of the problem depending on the value of s selected. In their work using the household budget surveys of European Community members, with poverty defined on an expenditure basis, de Vos and Zaidi find that:

> the ranking of the countries with respect to the overall poverty incidence is hardly affected when different equivalence scales are used. However, the composition of the poor population shows considerable changes ... The poverty incidence among specific household groups, such as single elderly and households with children, is particularly sensitive to the choice of equivalence scale. (1995a, p. 1)

Similarly, the study by Burkhauser et al. (1996) shows that, in comparisons of Germany and the United States, the composition of the poverty population is sensitive to the choice of equivalence scale.

The comparisons made above assume that the same equivalence scale should be applied in both countries, but the appropriate equivalence scale may vary from country to country. Where, for instance, the fixed costs of a household are relatively low, then standard of living considerations may point to a scale which is close to per capita. In another country, where fixed costs, such as those for housing, heating and property taxes, are relatively larger, then the costs of additional household members may be less, and we may want to take a lower value of s.

1.4 Differing Judgements and Dominance Criteria

The welfare economics heritage of economics has in many ways been a stultifying one, with its emphasis on Pareto efficiency and our inability to go beyond individual welfare as a criterion. However, there is one valuable contribution, which is the insistence on recognizing the diversity of social judgements and on the development of decision rules which seek to identify a minimum degree of common ground. This may be described in terms of 'dominance' criteria, which in the present context involves seeking to identify conditions under which we can say unambiguously that there is less poverty in one country than another. Such an idea is of course far from new. It is common practice to take a range of poverty lines: for example, poverty criteria of 40 per cent, 50 per cent and 60 per cent of average income. But what economists have done is to consider systematically what is involved in this approach and to develop the tools which can be used to apply such dominance ideas.

The need to take account of such differences in views is illustrated by three sources of disagreement: the location of the poverty line, relation between poverty and inequality, and choice of poverty measure.

Differences in judgement about the poverty line

That differences in social judgements are likely to arise is evident in the case of the minimum rights approach, but they also arise with the standard of living formulation. Starting from a set of basic needs, there is room for considerable disagreement about the subsistence standard, x^*. Even in the case of food requirements, where a physiological basis may appear to provide a firm starting point, it is difficult to determine x^* with any precision. There is no single level of food intake required to survive, but rather a broad range where physical efficiency declines with a falling intake of calories and protein. Nutritional needs depend on where people live and on what they are doing. They vary from person to person, so that any statement can only be probabilistic. In the case of non-food items, there is even greater scope for judgement. This applies whether we seek to include the goods in the vector x^* or whether we allow for non-food items via the multiplier h, as in equation (1.2).

The range of possible poverty lines is well illustrated by the studies of Herman Deleeck and colleagues (for example, Deleeck et al. (1992) and Van den Bosch et al. (1993)) which have examined the implications of the EC poverty line, of a legal poverty line (guaranteed minimum income), and for two subjective standards (the CSP poverty line devised by the Centre for Social Policy (CSP), Antwerp, and the Subjective Poverty Line (SPL) following the Leyden approach. The subjective standards are based on the survey question 'what is the minimum amount of income that your family, in your circumstances, needs to be able to make ends meet?'. The responses tend to rise less than 1 to 1 with actual income, starting above actual income. A regression line fitted to the responses, taking account of family characteristics, gives a level of income where they coincide with actual income, and this is the basis for the SPL standard. The CSP method makes use of a second question which asks people how they 'get by' with their current income. Those responding 'with some difficulty' are assumed to be just balancing their budgets, and their responses to the minimum income question, again distinguished by family type, are used to calculate the CSP standard. (The underlying assumptions can, of course, be challenged.[22]) The resulting poverty

---

[22] For a critique of the Leyden approach in general, see Seidl (1994); for a vigorous reply, see van Praag and Kapteyn (1994).

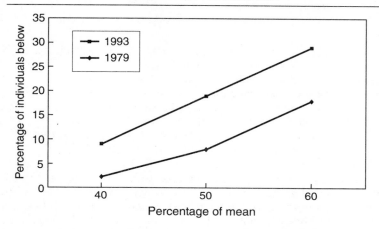

Figure 1.8 Dominance criterion: UK 1979 and 1993/4.
Source: Department of Social Security (1996), table F1.

lines are substantially higher than the EU standard. For a couple
with 1 child in Belgium in 1985, the SPL line is 28 per cent higher
and the CSP line is 37 per cent higher. The SPL line is nearly twice
that based on the legal minimum.

It therefore makes sense to consider a range of poverty lines. Suppose that π_{min} is the lowest poverty line that anyone considers possible and that π_{max} is the highest. A natural way to proceed is to say
that we can make an unambiguous comparison of two situations (say
UK in 1993 with the UK is 1979) if the number in poverty is lower in
one case for all possible poverty lines between π_{min} and π_{max}. If we
write the cumulative distribution of income (or expenditure) as $F(Y)$
in the final year and $F^*(Y)$ in the initial year, and use $\Delta F(Y)$ to
denote the difference, $F(Y)-F^*(Y)$, then we require for $F(Y)$ to domi-
nate $F^*(Y)$ that

$$\Delta F(\pi) \leq 0 \quad \text{for all } \pi \text{ belonging to the range } [\pi_{min}, \pi_{max}] \quad (1.4)$$

In this exposition, I ignore differences in population size and nor-
malize so that $F(Y)$ is the *proportion* of the population with incomes
equal or less than Y. The application of the *restricted dominance*
criterion (1.4) is illustrated in figure 1.8 where the range of possible
poverty lines is taken from 40 to 60 per cent of the mean. (In the
figure 1.8, income is expressed relative to the mean.) The curve for
1979 lies everywhere below that for 1993. Reversing the condition
(1.4), indicates that 1979 dominates 1993/4 in that the conclusion
will be accepted by people who are not necessarily in agreement on
the precise location of the poverty line but who agree that it lies

[43]

between 40 and 60 per cent of the average (and agree on a relative measure).

This dominance procedure can be a most useful one, but it is important to note two features. The first is that it provides only a *ranking*. We can draw a conclusion about the direction of change but not about the quantitative magnitude. The second is that the ranking is only a *partial* one. There may well be situations where the curves intersect, in which case we cannot reach any conclusion.

What can we do if the dominance condition is not satisfied? One possible direction of progress is suggested by the observation that (1.4) is a *first-degree* dominance condition. In the literature on inequality measurement (for example, Atkinson, 1970), the set of possible rankings has been increased by moving from first-degree to *second-degree* dominance. Suppose that one curve starts off ahead, in that there are fewer people with really low incomes. We may then feel that this gives it an advantage which persists beyond the point of intersection, since it has less 'serious' poverty. What this means is that there is a smaller *poverty deficit*, where the poverty deficit curve is defined for a specified poverty line, π:

$$G(\pi) \equiv \int_0^\pi [\pi - Y] f(Y) \, dY \tag{1.5}$$

where $f(Y)$ denotes the density function. Since we can also write[23]

$$\Delta G(\pi) \equiv \int_0^\pi \Delta F(Y) \, dY \tag{1.6}$$

it follows that, if $\Delta F(Y)$ is negative for all values of Y below π, then the poverty deficit is certainly smaller; given continuity, the same continues to be true for some range of higher poverty lines. We can apply the *second-degree restricted dominance* condition, which requires that

$$\Delta G(\pi) \leq 0 \text{ for all } \pi \text{ belonging to the range } [\pi_{\min}, \pi_{\max}] \tag{1.7}$$

Where the poverty deficit is smaller for all relevant poverty lines, then we can unambiguously say that there has been an improvement.

It should be noted that these are *restricted* dominance conditions, required to hold only over the relevant range of poverty lines. As a result, they do not have the same properties as global conditions. The first-degree condition does not imply the second-degree condition, since the cumulative frequency may have been 'worse' below $\pi_{\min}$. Nonetheless, we may expect the second-degree condition in gen-

23 Taking the difference, and integrating by parts (see Atkinson, 1987).

eral to allow a wider range of rankings. This is illustrated in Atkinson (1987) by data for the United States in 1974, 1979 and 1982. The cumulative frequencies for 1974 and 1979 intersect at the official poverty line, so that we cannot reach agreement if some people hold that the poverty line should be lower and others that it should be higher. However, the poverty deficit for 1974 is lower, so that we have second-degree dominance for a range of poverty lines above the official cut-off.

Poverty and Inequality

The poverty deficit is related to the Lorenz curve used in income inequality analysis (for further discussion see Shorrocks, 1995, and Sen and Foster, 1997). Suppose that for two distributions we have identical percentages below the poverty line, assumed to be expressed as a proportion of the mean, then if the Lorenz curve for distribution A lies above that of distribution B at all lower levels of income, then the poverty deficit is smaller. This is illustrated in figure 1.9, where the poverty deficit (divided by the mean) is given by the vertical distance between the point P and the Lorenz curve. The deficit is larger for the distribution B than for the distribution A.[24]

This reference to the Lorenz curve leads us to ask about the relation between *poverty* and *inequality*. Confronted in 1989 with the European Community statistics on poverty, the British Prime Minister, Mrs Thatcher, responded by saying that the Commission was confusing 'poverty' and 'inequality'. According to her, 'poverty no longer exists in Britain, only inequality' and the European Commission study 'measured inequality, not poverty' (*Guardian*, 1 June 1989). Nor is this view confined to politicians. Commenting on the proposal of Victor Fuchs cited earlier to use half median income as a poverty line, Gary Fields (1980) says that:

> this is more an inequality measure than a poverty measure, because if everyone's income were to increase by the same percentage, poverty would be unaffected. (1980, p. 29)

'Is poverty different from inequality?' is a serious question, and in seeking an answer one does not find a great deal of assistance in the

---

24 It should be noted that the situation shown in figure 1.9 is a special one, in that the distributions have the same poverty counts. In general, the comparison of two distributions at the *same poverty line* will involve comparing points with different x-co-ordinates (i.e. one will be to the left or right of the other in the Lorenz curve diagram).

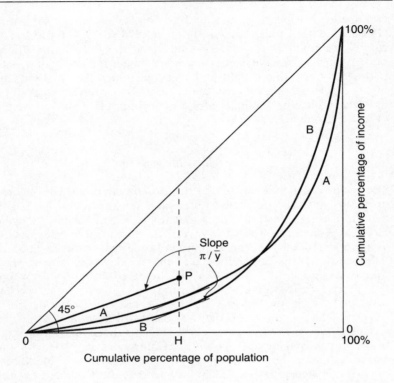

Figure 1.9 Lorenz curve and poverty deficit: special case where headcounts identical.

literature. People write about both inequality and poverty but in different articles or books and tend not to make the connection. I am myself guilty in this respect.

What kind of response can one give? There are of course those who agree with Mrs Thatcher, although she might be surprised in some cases by their identity. There are people belonging to the egalitarian left who regard concern with poverty as distracting attention from the more basic inequalities. Poverty is simply a manifestation of more general injustice. On the other hand, there are people who are concerned with both poverty and inequality and find it useful to distinguish between them. In order to see how they are related, I find it helpful to think in terms of the distributional weights, or *marginal valuation of income*, applied to the income received by different groups. Distributional weights may be familiar from their use in investment

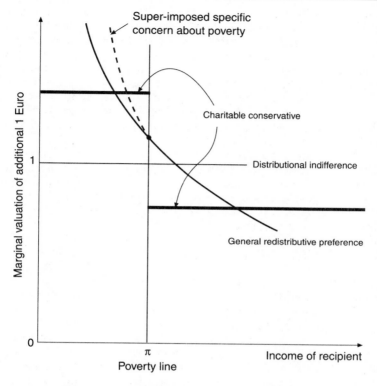

Figure 1.10 Different approaches to marginal
valuation of income.

appraisal. In figure 1.10, we measure income along the horizontal
axis and the marginal valuation of an additional Euro on the vertical. Then the light horizontal line corresponds to the case of distributional indifference: we give the same weight (1) to 1 Euro whoever
receives it. On the other hand, an evaluator who has a general concern for redistribution will have a set of weights which decline in
some systematic way with income, like the curve shown in figure
1.10. This would correspond to a concern about inequality of the
type just described, where no specific significance is attached to any
particular income level. An equalizing transfer from a person to some-
one less well-off would be regarded as desirable at all points in the
distribution.

Suppose, however, that people are specifically concerned about the
lower part of the income range, identifying a poverty line, π. Families

with incomes below the poverty line are regarded as being 'deserving', and are given more weight. They are regarded as having more need for a marginal Euro. But this concern with the poor may go together with distributional indifference above the poverty line; above π the line is horizontal as shown. Where the marginal valuation is constant below the poverty line, and the average marginal valuation is equal to 1, then we have the combination marked by the heavy line in figure 1.10. I have described this position elsewhere (Atkinson, 1995) as that of a 'charitable conservative' and it may be iden-tified as being held by some of Mrs Thatcher's supporters.

A third version is where specific concern for poverty is combined with a more general redistributive weighting, as illustrated by the dashed addition to the general redistributive preference curve in figure 1.10. It could, for example, be that the marginal valuation falls with the square root of income once the poverty line π is passed, but that greater weight is attached to incomes the further they are below the poverty line, as indicated by the dashed curve. In this way, we have combined concern with poverty and that for inequality, but the considerations which enter the two elements may be different. The arguments which lead to a particular shape of the general curve may be different from those which apply to the dashed specific poverty part. For example, I find Amartya Sen's reasoning with regard to the Gini coefficient, relating the marginal valuation of income to a person's rank in the distribution (Sen, 1974), quite persuasive in the case of the general curve (and hence when measuring income inequality), but not convincing when it comes to the specific poverty component. For this reason, I am not a partisan of the Sen version of the poverty index (Sen, 1976) – although I fully accept that one should be concerned about the distribution among the poor, which brings me to the choice of poverty measure.

Choice of poverty measure

There has been a large literature on the choice of poverty measure, stimulated by the article of Sen (1976). One of the main contributions of this article was to call into question the widespread use of the headcount measure – like the statistic of 50 million poor in the European Community. According to Sen, the degree of support commanded by this measure is 'quite astonishing' (1976, p. 295), and in the 1960s Harold Watts had said that 'it had little but its simplicity to recommend it' (1968, p. 326).

The obvious objection to the headcount is that it gives no indication of the severity of poverty: people may be close to the poverty line or far below. The properties of the head count may be seen from considering the marginal valuation of income implied by use of the headcount. Clearly a marginal 1 Euro contributes zero if it goes to a person above the poverty line. But it is also zero if it goes to people more than 1 Euro below the line, since it still leaves them below and the poverty count is unchanged. The value is only positive in the range of 1 Euro below the poverty line: we have a spike. The implied marginal valuation of income is very ill-behaved. With the head-count, the marginal valuation of income is not everywhere a decreasing function of income. Not only does the measure not respond to apparently beneficial changes – like giving a Euro to a really poor person – but it may have a perverse response to an equalizing transfer. Equalizing transfers play a key role in the theory of inequality measurement and the assumption is commonly made that the transfer of 1 Euro from a richer person to a poorer person is an improvement (or at least does not worsen the distribution), referred to as the *transfer principle*.[25] Yet this transfer would raise the head-count if the donor were above the poverty line, but by less than 1 Euro, and the recipient were below by more than 1 Euro.

For this reason, the theoretical literature has developed alternatives to the head-count. Before however going on to consider these alternative measures, I should enter a defence of the head-count. The welfare economic argument is one that fits with the standard of living approach to poverty, but on a minimum rights approach the head-count may be more defensible. If a minimum income is a basic right, then the head-count measures the number deprived of that right. It is indeed an either/or condition. A minimum rights approach to the measurement of poverty may therefore lead us to adopt the simple headcount, despite its undesirable properties from a welfare standpoint. This, however, raises the problem of the relationship with inequality measurement. In Atkinson (1987), I proposed a lexicographic approach, inspired by the two principles of justice of Rawls (1971). The first principle, which has priority, is concerned with basic liberties, and I suggested that, in terms of economic resources, this could be interpreted as being secured by the right to a minimum level of income. Poverty comes first, but inequality enters the assessment as a second concern (in Rawls' case this is the difference principle). On this lexicographic approach, there would be no requirement to use the same form of measure. It would be quite consistent to use the head-count to measure poverty and a measure satisfying the transfer principle for inequality.

Having said this, I am now going to assume that the poverty measure is consistent with the assumption that the marginal valuation of

25 Although the transfer principle can be challenged – see Amiel and Cowell (1996).

income declines with income, thus excluding the head-count. (I am also assuming that the marginal valuation of income may be meaningfully defined: for example that the measure is additively separable.) What then are the candidates? The first is the poverty deficit, to which I have already referred, which is the sum (integral) of the shortfall from the poverty line. The marginal value of a Euro is then 1 for all incomes below the poverty line. The poverty deficit has been normalized in various ways. The poverty deficit divided by the poverty line (G/π) is often referred to as the *poverty gap*. The poverty deficit divided by (π multiplied by the poverty population) is a measure of the *intensity* of poverty:

$$I \equiv G \,/\, \pi \, F(\pi) \tag{1.8}$$

The poverty deficit in turn may be criticized for evaluating equally all transfers to people below the poverty line irrespective of the seriousness of their poverty. The measure is indifferent to transfers between two people on the same side of the poverty line. For this reason, more sophisticated measures have been suggested, which have a declining marginal valuation below the poverty line, so that a transfer from a person close to the poverty line to a person far below the line has the effect of reducing measured poverty. For example, there is the class of measures proposed by Foster, Greer and Thorbecke (1984) (referred to below as the FGT measures), which take a power of the poverty gap, as indicated in the formula

$$P_a{}^a \equiv \int_0^\pi \left[(\pi - Y)/\pi\right]^a f(Y)\, dY \qquad \text{where } a > 0 \tag{1.9}$$

If $a = 1$, then the left-hand side is the poverty deficit, normalized by π, and higher values of a give greater weight to larger poverty gaps. The marginal valuation of income implied by the right-hand side of (1.9) is plotted in figure 1.11 for three different values of a. The value $a = 1$ implies that the same value is attached to a marginal 1 Euro at all income levels below the poverty line. The value $a = 2$ gives a linearly declining marginal valuation; higher values, such as that of $a = 3$ shown, give a non-linear decline in the marginal valuation, with more weight attached to additional income given to the very poorest. As the parameter a rises more and more weight is attached to the lowest income levels. Another argument for the use of this measure is provided by Ravallion (1994) in terms of measurement error: where income is measured with error, we may want to consider a wider range of incomes and a smoother measure even if our concern is solely with the worst-off person.

The problem is now that people have different values of a, or they

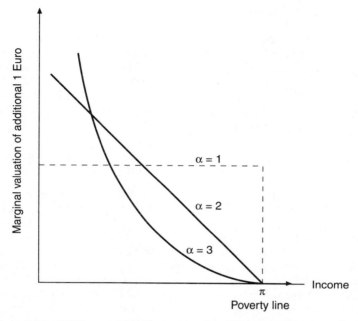

Figure 1.11 FGT measures of poverty with different parameter values.

may want to adopt a different type of measure. How can such differences be allowed for? Following the approach described earlier, we should not seek to persuade people to adopt our own particular measures – at least once we are sure that they fully understand the implications of their choice. Rather we should seek to identify circumstances in which there may be agreement despite disagreement. Can we derive dominance conditions that indicate that one situation is preferred to another for all measures in a specified class?

As I have shown elsewhere (Atkinson, 1987), if we restrict attention to the class of additively separable poverty measures, then we can apply a vari-ation of the dominance conditions described above. The dominance conditions allow us to make a ranking irrespective of the choice of either poverty measure or poverty line. (We get two choices for the price of one!) If the poverty measure is such that the marginal valuation is welldefined and is non-increasing with income (including the case where it is constant over some range) then a sufficient condition for there to be less poverty is that the poverty deficit curve lie below (or not above) for all income levels up to the poverty line (the lowest observed income is assumed to be zero):

$\Delta G(\pi) \leq 0$ for all π belonging to the range $[0, \pi_{max}]$ (1.7′)

Comparing this condition with (1.7), we can see that it is stronger in that the inequality has to hold at *all* income levels below a_{max}, and not just those considered possible poverty lines. It is also important to note that the conditions on the marginal valuation of income rule out the head-count, which is not covered by this condition. Nonetheless, the dominance condition is quite powerful, and is readily checked, which makes it a useful tool.

Concluding Comment

At the heart of many of the problems are differences in social judgements. I have emphasized the way in which dominance results can be used to reach a limited degree of agreement. At the same time, there may be limits to its application. We may not be able to narrow down the range of measures considered to the class for which dominance applies. It is noteworthy for example that the head-count – excluded from the dominance condition – continues to enjoy great popularity, perhaps because it is readily transparent, or because poverty, as suggested above, is really seen as an either/or condition. Or the dominance conditions may be regarded by some people as too demanding to be useful. We may therefore have to think hard about the choices to be made. One useful ingredient in such a reflection is to consider the practice of different countries. The studies reviewed in the next section are of interest not just for their substantive findings but also for the light they cast on the issues of definition.

1.5 National Studies of Poverty

In this section, I describe a selection of national studies of economic/financial poverty, by which I mean studies of individual Member States often, although not invariably, carried out by official bodies such as the Commissione di indagine sulla povertà e sull'emarginazione in Italy, or INSEE in France, or the Department of Social Security in the United Kingdom. The studies are treated in turn country by country, for ten of the fifteen Member States of the European Union, and the main conclusions are summarized at the end.

In each case, I begin by describing briefly the main features of the different sources of evidence in the country in question. (More detail is given in the Appendix.) I then present the main findings. It should be emphasized that the national estimates of the level of poverty are not comparable across countries. There are major differences in the sources and methods. For instance, although in each case results are given for the EC standard of 50 per cent of the average, this can be interpreted differently, as we have seen in section 1.1, and countries have also applied different poverty standards, such as those based on subjective evaluations of poverty. The coverage of national studies differs considerably across countries. For some countries, there are data for every year; in others the relevant survey is only carried out twice a decade. For some countries, we have to rely on a single source of information. For others, there is more than one source, and these are not necessarily comparable. I should also stress that I have not attempted to be comprehensive in this review. Not all European Union countries are covered (the omissions are Austria, Denmark, Greece, Portugal and Spain),[26] and there are important studies within the remaining ten which are omitted.

To these reservations must be added the obvious fact that all data are measured with error. We may arrive at a misleadingly high proportion of people below the poverty line on account of income understatement, or because we have failed to ask about a component of income. The figure may be misleadingly low if there is a lower response rate to the survey among poor households, or if benefits are imputed to people who do not in fact receive them. Even if there are no sources of bias, sample estimates are subject to sampling error, and ideally confidence intervals would be given for all estimates. In the case of the EC standard, this involves the sampling properties both of the distribution and of the poverty cut-off (50% of the sample mean). As is pointed out by Preston (1993), these may interact to reduce the sampling error (below that with a fixed poverty cut-off). His calculations for the United Kingdom suggest a 95 per cent confidence interval for the proportion below the EC standard of about ± 0.8 percentage points; the 'approximate' figure given by the Department of Social Security (1996, p. 211) is ±1.3 percentage points.[27] We have also to consider the robustness of the poverty estimates to (possibly a few) extreme observations.[28]

---

26 For evidence on poverty in Denmark, see, among others, Hallöräd et al. (1996), on Greece, see Tsakloglou (1990) and Petmesidou (1996), on Portugal, see Silva (1992) and da Costa (1994), and on Spain, see Ruiz-Castillo (1987), Mercader-Prats (1993 and 1997), and Cantó-Sânchez (1996).
27 For further discussion of sampling errors, see Kakwani (1993) and Preston (1993); Jäntti (1992) considers methods of statistical inference for poverty dominance criteria.
28 Cowell and Victoria-Feser (1996) examine the implications of data contamination using the tool of the *influence function*. Their results show that for a fixed poverty line the poverty measures studied here (the FGT class) are robust to a small proportion of arbitrary extreme observations, but this is not guaranteed when the poverty line depends on the mean income (whereas it would be if the poverty line were based on the median).

There are two main questions on which attention is focused. The first is the comparison of recent *trends in financial poverty over time*. The massive rise in unemployment in Europe since the 1970s would lead one to expect poverty to have increased substantially, reinforced by increased segmentation of the labour market, growing insecurity of employment, and cut-backs in state spending on social transfers. Demographically, there has been an increase in the number of one-parent families, and in the number of the very old. In the opposite direction, the fall in the number of large families may have reduced the poverty rate, and the financial impact of worsening labour market conditions may have been offset by increased participation by married women in paid employment. It is therefore of interest to establish how far financial poverty has in fact increased in Europe since the end of the 1970s. In considering what the national studies show about the trends, I also cross-refer to the results of Zaidi and de Vos (1996) for nine countries of the European Community in the 1980s using the Eurostat collection of household budget surveys.

The second main point is the relation of incomes to the *legal minimum* embodied in social assistance programmes. It is the avowed intention of such programmes that they ensure a minimum floor, and it is important to ask whether this safety net is effective. The findings are very relevant to the question of the 'take-up' of benefits, which is investigated in Lecture 2, and to the discussion of 'targeting' in Lecture 3. At the same time, it should be re-iterated that the figures are only estimates. The finding that x per cent of families are below the legal minimum may reflect limitations of the estimates: for example, the information contained in the survey may be less complete than that available to the local social security office. The survey may relate to a household unit, whereas the legal minimum applies to a smaller claimant unit, so that any extrapolation to the household has to be approximate.

Belgium

In Belgium, the household budget survey was used for the study by Hagenaars et al. (1994) and that by Zaidi and de Vos (1996). According to the latter, poverty measured on an expenditure basis, and applying the EC poverty standard of 50 per cent of the mean, increased from 4.7 per cent of persons in 1978–9 to 7.4 per cent in 1987–8. On the other hand, measured in terms of households, the increase was not significant: from 5.5 to 6.6 per cent.

Here, I concentrate on poverty measured on an income basis, drawing on the 1985, 1988 and 1992 waves of the Centre for Social Policy (CSP) panel survey, which covers all private households in

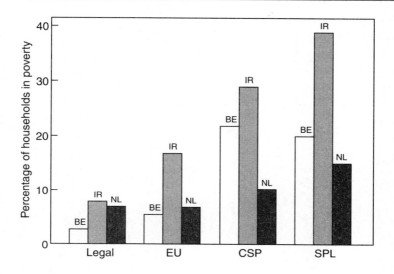

Figure 1.12   Poverty: different standards: Belgium 1988, Ireland 1987 and
Netherlands 1986.
Source: Deleeck et al. (1992), table 4.2.

Belgium. A range of different approaches has been used in Belgium
to the definition of the level of the poverty line, and a selection of
the findings for the overall extent of poverty are summarized in
figure 1.12, which covers also Ireland and the Netherlands (see below). According to the EC 50 per cent of mean income poverty line,
in 1985 (and 1988) about 6 per cent of households in Belgium were
living in poverty, a finding very close to that given in the previous
paragraph. The proportion who were regarded as poor according
to the legal minimum (Recht op Bestaansminimum, plus guaranteed child allowance) was about half this percentage, although it is
nonetheless striking that about 3 per cent of Belgian households
were below the social safety net level. As we have seen, much higher
standards, and poverty percentages around 20 per cent, are obtained using the subjective approaches to determining the poverty
line.

It is no surprise that the poverty count depends very much on the
poverty standard chosen; of more interest is the finding of Cantillon
et al. (1994) that the trend over time is different for different indicators. For the EC scale there is broad stability between 1985 and
1992 in the proportion of households below the poverty line, with

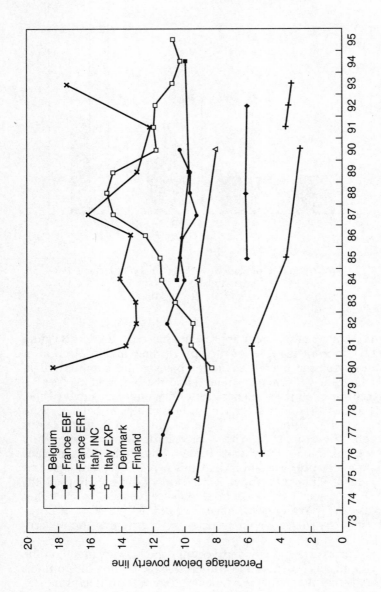

Figure 1.13 Poverty in European countries I.

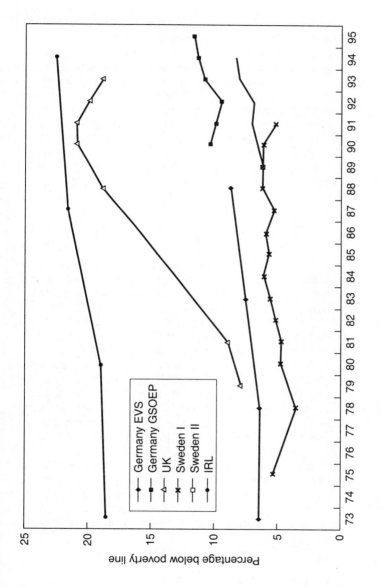

Figure 1.14 Poverty in European countries II.

the percentage varying only from 6.1 per cent in 1985 to 6.0 per cent in 1992. This is shown in figure 1.13. (figures 1.13 and 1.14 summarize results using the EC standard for different countries, although it should be noted that this is not always interpreted in the same way.) For the CSP poverty line (not shown) there is a sizeable reduction: from 21.4 per cent in 1985 to 17.6 per cent in 1992 (although no indication is given of the statistical significance). This does, however, reflect the fact that the subjective poverty line, which depends on the survey responses in different years, rose less sharply than average income. Between 1985 and 1992, average income, and hence the EC standard, rose by 16 per cent in real terms, whereas for a number of family types the subjective poverty line scarcely rose at all. This underlines the importance of the issue of up-rating of the poverty standard over time. Different approaches can lead to conclusions which are not only quantitatively but also qualitatively dissimilar.[29]

Finland

In Finland, data are available from household budget surveys, augmented by income information from tax returns and other official registers, and from income distribution surveys. Studies using these data include Uusitalo (1989), Gustafsson and Uusitalo (1990), and Ritakallio (1994). The estimates in figure 1.13 are from the work of Jäntti and Ritakallio (1996). They apply an EC standard, taken to be 50 per cent of median equivalent income using the OECD scale (so that in terms of our earlier case study in section 1.1, their estimate follows the French rather than the United Kingdom interpretation). The figures from 1976 to 1990 are from the household surveys; those from 1991 are from the income distribution statistics. There is therefore a break in the series. Overall, there appears to have been a decline in the poverty rate. (From 1966 to 1976 there had been a much more sharp decline.)

The poverty studies also apply a poverty line based on the national pension, which has been close to the guidelines for public assistance. As noted above, this line increased less in real terms, and the resulting decline in measured poverty is accordingly larger. According to Ritakallio, the poverty rate on this basis was no more than 1 per cent in 1990 (1994, p. 121).

29 Poverty in Belgium is surveyed in the recent study by Meulders et al. (1996); for a review in largely qualitative terms, see Fondation Roi Baudouin (1994).

France

In France, two major national sources have been used to assess the extent of low incomes: the household budget survey (EBF) employed by Hagenaars et al. (1994) and the fiscal survey (ERF). The results on income poverty, using disposable income after tax, and applying a standard of 50 per cent of the median, from the two sources (EBF and ERF), are summarized in figure 1.13.[30] As is explained by Assémat and Glaude (1989), we would expect the budget survey figures to be rather higher, in view of the disproportionate under-reporting of income, although the adjustments to the fiscal data, imputing means-tested benefits to all eligible recipients, may go too far in the opposite direction, since they ignore incomplete take-up of these benefits.

As far as trends over time are concerned, the figures show some variation from year to year, but the broad impression is that of stability. Bourguignon and Martinez (1996) show an upward trend in the proportion below 50 per cent of the mean (as opposed to the median in figure 1.13) between 1979 and 1984/5, but this does not continue to 1989. On the other hand, the Synthèses (1996) study finds little overall trend when poverty is defined in terms of before tax income and 50 per cent of the median.[31] Perhaps the most important factor is that the Synthèses (1996) study finds a rise in poverty among households with an active head (or a head aged less than 60) from 9.9 per cent in 1984 to 11.4 per cent in 1994, but a decline among other households (from 11.5 to 6.9 per cent). The sizeable reduction in the poverty rate for households headed by a pensioner has offset the rise in unemployment and a rise in the poverty rate among the employed.

The estimates of poverty by Zaidi and de Vos (1996) from the EBF, based on expenditure, show an increase, measured in terms of households, from 13.2 per cent in 1984–5 to 14.9 per cent in 1989. While statistically significant, the increase is relatively modest in size. Overall, the conclusions seems to be that, as far as income poverty in France is concerned, there do not appear to be dramatic movements at the aggregate level. There have nonetheless been significant differences between subgroups.

30 The ERF estimates are taken from a graph in the Synthèses (1995) study (p. 56). In comparing them with the results of Assémat and Glaude, it should be noted that figure 1.14 uses the full sample in each case (and therefore includes people not in the overlapping sample).
31 The use of before tax income affects both the evaluation of the situation of the low income household and the standard being applied (the position of the median).

Germany

The two main sources which have been used to measure poverty in Germany (the EVS budget survey and the GSOEP household panel) yield rather different results. Hauser and Semrau (1989) show that for 1983, an overlapping year, the poverty rate according to the EC standard was 6.1 per cent according to the EVS but more than twice as large (13.6 per cent) according to the panel survey. (Both figures relate to households with a German head.) This is a salutary warning that the choice of data and definition can make a major difference. Hauser and Semrau attribute the difference to the under-representation of low-income households in the EVS (which is not based on a random sample, but on a call for voluntary participation) and to differential under-reporting of income in the GSOEP. It may be noted that if we allow for households with a non-German head, the figure in GSOEP rises to 14.8 per cent (from 13.6 per cent).

The changes over time in the proportion in West Germany below the EC standard, as derived from the EVS and GSOEP by Becker (1996) and Hauser (1996) are given in figure 1.14.[32] There appears to have been a modest rise in poverty between 1978 and 1988. (The estimates based on expenditure of Zaidi and de Vos (1996) show a rise in poverty from 8.9 per cent of persons in 1983 to 9.7 per cent in 1988.) For the latter part of this period, 1983–6, the estimates of Hauser and Semrau (1989, table 11) from the GSOEP, not shown in figure 1.14, also suggest a rise in the poverty rate, of some 4 per centage points. The GSOEP panel is used by Hauser (1996) to produce the estimates for 1990–5 shown in figure 1.14, where there is again a modest overall increase. Judged by the EC standard, poverty in West Germany has increased to a noticeable if not dramatic extent. Hauser (1996, table 3) also provides results for the former East German Länder. Measured according to the EC standard the poverty rate in 1990 was only a third of that in West Germany (3.7 per cent), but it has risen to 8.0 per cent in 1995. Poverty has more than doubled.

In addition to the EC standard, the social assistance level has been used in a definition of 'combatted poverty' (those in receipt of assistance) and 'concealed poverty' (those eligible on the basis of

---

32 These employ a different equivalence scale. Whereas, Hauser and Semrau used a scale based on the *monetary* benefits under the social assistance law, the more recent estimates take account of the payment of rent and heating. The resulting scale is close to the OECD scale, which has therefore been used by Becker (1996) and Hauser (1996).

income, but not in receipt). The results of Hauser and Semrau (1990, p. 37) show that in 1983 1.3 per cent of the population were in concealed poverty and 2.6 per cent in receipt of social assistance. This indicates a take-up rate of two-thirds, but Hauser and Semrau (1989, table 10) argue that this is over-stated, since the recipients include those whose annual income (on which eligibility is based) is above the assistance scale (since they were only temporarily below).

Ireland

Studies of financial poverty in Ireland rely on household surveys, and the results shown in figure 1.14 make use of three such surveys, linking the results. For 1980 and 1987, Nolan and Whelan (1996) use the Household Budget Survey (HBS) for 1980 and the separate household survey carried out by the Economic and Social Research Institute (ESRI) for 1987. The latter in turn is compared by Nolan (1996) and Callan et al. (1996) with the data for 1994 collected in the first wave of the European Community Household Panel, referred to as the Living in Ireland Survey. The resulting estimates for Ireland of the proportion of persons below the EC standard are shown in figure 1.14. These indicate a rise in poverty, particularly in the 1980s. However, we have seen in the first section of this Lecture that the conclusions reached about the trend in poverty in Ireland depend on the definitions adopted. This is brought out clearly in the studies by Nolan and Whelan (1996), Nolan (1996) and Callan et al. (1996). As they show, the adoption of a household basis would show a fall in poverty between 1987 and 1994. This reflects a change in the composition of households below the poverty line: poor households tending to be larger. If we take the lower *40 per cent of mean income* standard, then the head-count of households falls substantially from 1987 to 1994. The shape of the distribution has changed, in the direction of a reduction in severe poverty.

The sensitivity of the poverty total to different approaches to defining the poverty line is illustrated in figure 1.12. As for Belgium, the legal minimum (discussed in more detail in the next paragraph) indicates a lower poverty count than the EC standard, and the subjective methods give much higher figures. Poverty on the SPL approach is four times that assessed according to the legal minimum.

The legal minimum is explored by Callan et al. (1989, p. 142), who show that in 1987 as many as 11.8 per cent of benefit units had incomes, after transfers, below the level of eligibility for the basic Supplementary Welfare Allowance (SWA), which is the safety-net social welfare scheme for those not eligible for other programmes.[33] Of these, some were ineligible for SWA: 3.1 per cent were in full-time education and 0.9 per cent were in full-time work. Some (2.2%) were in receipt of the SWA but less than the apparent entitlement. Of the remainder, 3.1 per cent appeared to be eligible but not claiming. The authors conclude that:

> Preliminary indications are that the social welfare system is failing to provide this minimal income to a significant proportion of the population. (Callan et al., 1989, p. 151)

Italy

There are two main national sources of data in Italy: the Bank of Italy sample survey of households, which can be used to measure income poverty, and the annual Istat survey of family budgets. The latter is the source for the main official poverty estimates, those of the Commissione di indagine sulla povertà e sull'emarginazione (1996), based on expenditure data and on the EC standard of 50 per cent of the mean. These are shown in figure 1.13 on an annual basis from 1980 to 1995. The headcount rose sharply from 8.3 per cent in 1980 to 14.8 per cent in 1988, but then declined, so that in 1995 it was 10.6 per cent, which is the same figure as in 1983. The estimates of Zaidi and de Vos (1996) based on expenditure show a rise from 1985 to 1988. Estimates have been produced using the Bank of Italy survey of income poverty by Cannari and Franco (1997), and these are also shown in figure 1.13. They differ noticeably for individual years, but both suggest that there was no marked upward trend over the period as a whole.

The Italian studies have devoted considerable attention to the intensity of poverty. This is measured by the average extent of shortfall, or the poverty gap divided by the (head-count × poverty line expressed relative to mean). This increased in the 1980s (Commissione di indagine sulla povertà e sull'emarginazione, 1996, Tav. 1): from 16 per cent in 1980 to 23 per cent in the mid-1980s, and remains around 20 per cent.

Luxembourg

In Luxembourg, the panel study of households (PSELL), dating from 1985, is used by Hausman (1995) to study the proportion of house-

---

33 The figure in figure 1.13 for the number below the legal minimum in Ireland provided by Deleeck et al. (1992) differs in that Deleeck et al. use the SWA rates to construct a *household* level poverty line, whereas Callan et al. (1989) look at the *tax/benefit unit* (which is the unit on which SWA is in general assessed).

holds who have resources below that which would make them eligible for the Revenu Minimum Garanti (RMG). This is therefore a legal poverty line. The proportion of households poor on this basis was 6.3 per cent in 1985, prior to the introduction of the RMG in 1986, but the figure has fallen since to 1.2 per cent in 1992. As is noted by Hausman, the fall came at a time of economic recovery, but in the early 1990s the RMG had an important role as a stabilizer. The fraction living below the legal minimum in the 1990s appears to be low by the standards of other countries.

Netherlands

The Socio-Economic Panel (SEP) of the Central Bureau of Statistics is the basis for the poverty studies cited here, including the figures already shown in figure 1.12 for the Netherlands in 1986. The proportion of households below the EC standard was 7.2 per cent (Deleeck et al., 1992, table 4.1 and Muffels et al., 1990, table 5.1). Interestingly, this is the same as with the legal minimum as a poverty standard, unlike the situation in Belgium and Ireland. The Netherlands is also dissimilar in that the CSP subjective poverty line does not lead to much higher poverty counts, and even with the SPL the poverty rate is only some twice that with the legal minimum. The impact of the choice of approach differs across countries.

Over time, the estimates presented by Dirven and Berghman (1992, table 2) suggest that the proportion of individuals (the figure in the previous paragraph is for households) below the legal poverty line increased from 6.5 per cent in 1986 to 9.2 per cent in 1988, and according to the subjective poverty line from 12.1 per cent to 14.7 per cent. The estimates based on expenditure of Zaidi and de Vos (1996) cover a longer period and show no significant rise from 1980 to 1988.

People could be living below the legal minimum for several reasons: benefits could have been reduced as a sanction for not satisfying the conditions of award, they could be students, or they could not be taking up their entitlement (van Oorschot, 1991). Whatever the reason,

> It appeared that the Dutch social protection system did not prevent that, in 1988, 9.2% of the Dutch population lived below the legal subsistence minimum. (Dirven and Berghman, 1992, p. 30)

Sweden

The annual Household Income Survey (HINK) provides the basis for the estimates of low incomes according to the EC standard (house-

[63]

holds below 50 per cent of the median) in the Swedish Ministry of Finance study (1996), from which results are shown in figure 1.14. At the end of the 1980s there was a revision of the method of calculating income, which leads to a break in the statistical series (the two parts being labelled I and II). Over the 1980s as a whole there was a modest upward trend. The rise from 1989 to 1994 was sharper: from 6.3 to 8.5 per cent.

The Ministry of Finance study compared household disposable income with the National Board of Health and Welfare's social assistance norm. In 1975 around 20 per cent of households were below the social assistance level, but this fell to 10 per cent by 1980 and remained around that figure for the decade. The report draws attention to the rise since 1990 (from 8.2% to 11.3% in 1994). It notes that there are a number of reasons why households may have incomes below the social assistance norm. They may have assets which debar them from entitlement; they may be self-employed for whom income is inaccurately measured; they may be students.

United Kingdom

In the United Kingdom, the main source that has been used to date to measure income poverty is the Family Expenditure Survey (FES), which underlies the Households Below Average Income estimates to which reference has already been made.[34] It is also the basis for the estimates of Hagenaars et al. (1994). The proportion below the EC standard according to the official HBAI series is shown in figure 1.14 (a similar series is given by Goodman and Webb, 1994). As we have already seen in section 1.2, the proportion below 50 per cent of the mean fell in the 1970s, but increased sharply in the 1980s, particularly after the middle of the decade. The estimates show a rise from 7.5 per cent in 1975 to more than 20 per cent in 1990. There is a slight fall in the early 1990s, but this is nowhere large enough to reverse the big rise from 1984 to 1989 when poverty doubled in five years. As figure 1.8 demonstrates, the finding of a large increase between 1979 and 1993/4 is not sensitive to the precise choice of poverty line: 40 per cent or 60 per cent of the mean give a similar picture. The increase is more than an order of magnitude larger than the standard errors (around 0.4 percentage points) estimated by Preston (1993).

34 As notes earlier, these estimates have been heavily criticized by Pryke (1995). His alternative estimate for 1988 for 1988 is only a third of the HBAI figure (6.4% of the population compared with 18.5%). It is not however possible to establish from his work how far poverty increased over time.

An alternative measure of the extent of income poverty is provided by a comparison with the minimum income guaranteed by social assistance: Income Support (previously Supplementary Benefit). Official estimates (Department of Health and Social Security, 1988 and 1988a) showed that in 1985 4.5 per cent of the population were living on incomes below the Supplementary Benefit (SB) level (excluding those in receipt of SB). In part, this is due to those not covered by the provisions, in particular those in full-time work and those disqualified (for example, on grounds of 'voluntary' unemployment). In part this is due to the non-take-up of assistance.

Conclusions

The first conclusion which can be drawn from these studies is that the results are sensitive to the precise definitions and methods adopted. This has, I trust, justified the emphasis placed on these conceptual issues in this Lecture. It also has implications for the discussion of policy alternatives in Lecture 3. If we cannot agree on the definition of poverty, and the results are sensitive to the choice of definition, then this does not augur well for solutions based on 'targeting' resources on the poor. In order to concentrate resources, we have to be able to identify the target population.

What, bearing in mind this qualification, can we conclude substantively? Several findings are suggested as far as the EC poverty standard is concerned:

(1)   The United Kingdom stands out for its sharp rise in the second part of the 1980s in the proportion with incomes less than 50 per cent of the mean (a rise of more than 10 percentage points), which has not been reversed;

(2)   Other countries have seen a rise in poverty, such as those shown in figure 1.14, like West Germany and Sweden, but it was much more modest: an increase of some 3–4 percentage points between 1978 and the mid-1990s; and

(3)   There are a number of European countries where there was little upward trend over the period as a whole, such as Belgium, Finland, and France (see figure 1.13), even if there may have been periods when poverty increased.

It is interesting to compare these findings with those of Van den Bosch and Marx (1996) and of Bradshaw and Chen (1996), both of whom make extensive use of the Luxembourg Income Study (LIS) database. According to the former:

[65]

Sharply rising trends in poverty were found in two countries (Ireland and the UK), while modest increases in poverty were measured in a number of other countries, including Australia, Germany, France, Sweden and the USA. In several countries, poverty has remained stable, or even declined. (Van den Bosch and Marx, 1996, pp. 21–2)

The findings here differ for France and Ireland, where I am considering more recent periods, but the general picture is not dissimilar. According to Bradshaw and Chen, poverty more than doubled in the United Kingdom, increased in Germany, but showed more modest or no changes in the Netherlands, Norway and Sweden.

As has been pointed out by Cantillon (1992) in the case of Belgium, the stability in aggregate indicators of financial poverty in a number of countries contrasts with the frequent references to increasing social duality and the rise of 'new poverty'. In part, the stability may result from the balancing of different forces, some of which (such as the macro-economic situation and the rise in single-parent families) have increased poverty, others of which (such as the rise in the number of women working in the paid labour force, better pensions, and the fall in the number of large families) have had the reverse effect. In part, the difference is because I am concerned here with financial poverty, whereas other dimensions, identified by those writing about new poverty, may have seen an increase.

The final conclusion is that there are several countries where there is evidence that an important minority of the population are living below the legal minimum, that is the income floor set by the social assistance system. We have seen this to be the case in Belgium, Ireland, the Netherlands, Sweden, the United Kingdom and West Germany. The failure to ensure the chosen legal minimum, which of course varies from country to country, indicates, at least at first sight, a shortfall in the effectiveness of social policy. Although there are other explanations, including errors of measurement, one aspect – explored in the next two Lectures – is the failure of people to claim benefits to which they are entitled.

Concluding Comment to Lecture 1

In this Lecture I have emphasized the problems with the measurement of the extent of poverty in present-day Europe. The definition of poverty poses conceptual issues of some subtlety and its translation into concrete statistics is a major challenge. Indeed you may have the impression that I have raised more questions than I have answered. In the next Lecture I ask how far economic analysis may help in providing answers.

[66]

Lecture 2

Economics of Poverty, Unemployment and Social Exclusion

In seeking to understand the persistence of poverty in the countries of the European Union – countries which are rich and growing richer – there are two major lines of inquiry. First, there is the impact of the working of the economy, on the economic circumstances of individuals and on the way in which we view those circumstances. What have been the implications of jobless growth and the high unemployment which has characterized much of Europe in recent decades? Are there reasons why some people have not shared in rising prosperity? Is it that we have moved the goalposts, adopting a relative approach to the measurement of poverty? If so, are there good economic reasons for adjusting the poverty criterion in an age of rising living standards?

The second set of questions concern the determination and effect of government policy. Is poverty in rich countries the result of their macro-economic policies? Has the priority given to reducing inflation, or to cutting taxes, been responsible for the problem of poverty? If the answer is 'yes', then this raises the question as to why social policy has not been able to compensate the poor? Why has social transfer policy failed to eliminate financial poverty? Is it because policies are insufficiently targeted? In an increasingly globalised world, national governments may be limited in their freedom to carry out redistributive policy. Does this mean that action is necessary at the European level?

This Lecture is concerned with the first set of questions: the working of the economy (the next Lecture is about the political economy of poverty and the impact of government policy) and the question – What can economics contribute to the study of poverty? Can economic analysis clarify the conceptual issues which we have seen to arise in the definition of poverty and help us understand its persistence? Poverty is a subject to which other disciplines have made major contributions. Indeed, there are those who call into question the competence of economists in a field which they regard as largely sociological or political. However, while I would certainly acknowledge the importance of non-economic factors, I argue that economics has useful things to say.

A second theme that links the five sections of this Lecture is the triangular relationship between poverty, unemployment and social exclusion. In considering the economic causes of poverty, one thinks immediately of the labour market, and particularly of unemployment, and this is the subject of sections 2.1 and 2.2. Where social transfers replace less than 100 per cent of previous earnings, a rise in unemployment can cause a rise in financial poverty. How far it does so is the subject of section 2.1, where I start from the experience of the United States and see how far it is applicable to the European Union. The relation depends on, among other factors, the extent to which the unemployed live in households where there are other sources of income. It is conceivable that these other sources of income are sufficient to prevent unemployment leading to poverty. However, there are still good reasons to be concerned about unemployment. In Europe, these are often presented in terms of unemployment leading not only to poverty but also to *social exclusion*, a term that has come to be widely used, but whose exact meaning is not always clear. Indeed, it seems to have gained currency *because* it has no precise definition and means all things to all people. A review of the sociological literature concluded that:

> Observers in fact only agree on a single point: the impossibility to define the status of the 'excluded' by a single and unique criterion. Reading numerous enquiries and reports on exclusion reveals a profound confusion amongst experts. (Weinberg and Ruano-Borbalan, 1993, translation by Silver, 1995, p. 59)

What is agreed, however, is that social exclusion goes beyond lack of resources. Unemployment is a source of concern because people are financially worse off but also because it leads to social isolation and to estrangement from the economic system.

Different economic explanations of unemployment are the subject of section 2.2. A variety of theories are considered, with varying degrees of applicability to different countries (for example, the strength of trade unions varies across EU members, and some countries, like the United Kingdom, do not have minimum wages), which may help us understand the role of external macro-economic shocks and of internal labour market mechanisms. These explanations are important not just in understanding the causes of unemployment but also in evaluating the *process* by which it is generated. This is highly relevant to social exclusion, where there does seem to be agreement that exclusion is both a *state* and a *process*. The reasons why a person is unemployed may be important in addition to the fact that he or she is out of work. It is often alleged that people are 'voluntarily' unemployed by their own agency, rejecting job offers. This is a quite different situation from one where employers do not find it profitable to make job offers to people with no qualifications; and that in turn is different from one where it is illegal to offer jobs below a minimum wage.

The concern of the European with social exclusion is largely expressed in terms of unemployment, but social exclusion is not simply a question of what happens in the labour market. One of the main aims of this Lecture is to bring out the economic forces behind exclusion from *consumption*, and the way in which this may result from government policies. Exclusion from consumption activities leads to a weakening of social ties (Paugam, 1996; Strobel, 1996); these in turn rebound on the labour market but the consumption implications themselves are of great importance. Here attention is usually focused on households. They are certainly one side of the market; supplying labour to, and buying goods and services, from firms. But the other side of the market is also significant, as is emphasized in sections 2.3 and 2.4. The conditions under which goods are supplied is an aspect which is overlooked in the analysis of poverty. The decisions of firms about the prices and availability of products determine whether or not the poor are excluded from consumption. Modelling this interaction throws light on the risks of such exclusion and on the role played by government policy, such as the regulation of utility companies. The exclusion approach can moreover inform us about the way in which the poverty line should be adjusted over time. How do rising living standards affect the ability of the poor to participate in consumption? We are therefore brought back to the side of the triangle that links social exclusion to poverty. The two concepts are not to be equated, but they are related.

Decision-making by households is developed further in section 2.5, drawing on the micro-economics of household production. This provides a framework within which to clarify the distinction between absolute and relative poverty lines. Extending the analysis to introduce the allocation of time allows us to distinguish between people who are 'money poor' and those who are 'time poor'. This in turn casts light on the phenomenon of the incomplete take-up of benefits, which is one reason for people living below the legal minimum. It may be economically rational for a harassed lone parent in Britain to decide that he or she does not have the time required to study the ten-page instruction book for Family Credit. It is also possible that he or she finds the process of claiming or receipt to be demeaning or stigmatizing. This is yet another form of exclusion. In this case, the process by which people are excluded is the operation of the welfare state itself.

2.1 Macro-economics of Unemployment and Poverty

Economics students in the 1960s were taught about the Phillips curve 'trade-off' between unemployment and inflation. As illustrated in figure 2.1, governments could choose from a menu which offered lower unemployment at the expense of higher inflation or vice versa. The same is taught to undergraduates in the 1990s in terms of a *short-run trade-off*: for example, Mankiw tells students that 'the policymaker can depress aggregate demand to raise unemployment and lower inflation' (1994, p. 308). He refers to the 'sacrifice ratio', which is the percentage of a year's GDP which has to be sacrificed to reduce inflation by 1 percentage point, a typical estimate being about 5. Applying Okun's Law, which says that GDP and unemployment change in a ratio of around 2 to 1, Mankiw deduces that a 1 percentage point reduction in inflation requires 2H percentage points of unemployment for a year.

In the United States, there has been extensive research on the distributional implications of different choices from this trade-off frontier. In the 1970s the reasons for this investigation were obvious:

> If there is a stable long-run tradeoff between reducing inflation and reducing involuntary unemployment, macroeconomic decisions on the direction of the economy will in large part depend on the relative costs of benefits of achieving each objective. Any impact that inflation or unemployment has on the distribution of income should be a major factor in these calculations. (Gramlich, 1974, pp. 293–4)

Blank and Blinder (1986) estimated a time-series regression relating the United States poverty rate over the period 1959 to 1983 to the rates of unemployment and inflation, and to the ratio of transfers to Gross National product, and to the poverty line as a proportion of mean income. They found that:

> a 1-point rise in prime-age male unemployment raises the poverty rate by 0.7 points in the same year. If the rise in unemployment were sustained, the final net effect would be a 1.1-point rise . . . the effect of a 1-point rise in inflation is only one-seventh as large as that of a 1-point rise in unemployment. (1986, p. 188)

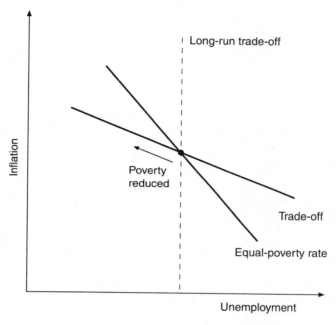

Figure 2.1 Inflation/unemployment trade-off.

The estimate of 1.1 percentage points relates to persons; the estimate for families is 0.97. In what follows I take for simplicity a figure of 1 percentage point rise in poverty for each 1 percentage point rise in unemployment. This relationship, it should be stressed, relates to the period prior to 1983; subsequently, it does not appear to hold (Blank, 1993), a matter to which I return in the next section. The slope of the trade-off between unemployment and inflation implied by this relationship is illustrated by the 'equal poverty rate' line shown in figure 2.1. If the journalists' 'misery index' is formed by adding the inflation and unemployment rates, the equal poverty rate criterion adds the unemployment rate to only one-seventh of the inflation rate.

There are two major problems with this 'classical' analysis of the distributional macro-economic trade-off. The first is with the macro-economics; the second is with the distributional evaluation. The macro-economics of the 1970s called into question the existence of a stable long-run 'Phillips curve'. As explained by Mankiw, the relationship described above is a short-run trade-off:

> Because people adjust their expectations of inflation over time, this tradeoff between inflation and unemployment holds only in the short run. . . . Eventually expectations adapt to whatever inflation rate the policymaker chooses. In the long run, . . . unemployment returns to its natural rate, and there is no tradeoff between inflation and unemployment. (Mankiw, 1994, p. 308)

In other words, the long-run relation is that shown by the dashed line in figure 2.1. The adjustment of people's expectations means, on this view, that government policy cannot permanently sustain a combination of non-accelerating prices and unemployment, other than at the so-called 'natural rate'. Since the poor are, according to the estimates of Blank and Blinder (1986), adversely affected by inflation, the long-run consequences of this policy are negative. Put differently, the dimension of the trade-off is different from that shown in figure 2.1 in that there is a continuing cost of inflation but a short-term benefit of lower unemployment.

It is not my intention here to consider the validity of these views, nor how long is the long run. To the extent, however, that there is a short-run trade-off, we need to consider whether the distributional implications in Europe are the same as those estimated for the United States. While economists often take it for granted that their conclusions can be shipped unmodified across the Atlantic, this is not necessarily the case.[1]

Unemployment and poverty in Europe

Unemployment in Europe in the early 1990s is around four times its level in the 1960s, and double that in the 1970s. The average unemployment rate (male and female) for the European Union was 4.6 per cent in 1974–9 and 9.4 per cent in 1990–3 (OECD, 1995, table 2.15). There are good grounds for expecting this to have led to a rise in poverty.

Rising unemployment can be expected to lead to increased overall poverty since the risk of poverty is greater for those who are unemployed than if they were in employment, either because they receive no transfers or because the transfers are not sufficient to bring them to the poverty line. Even in Continental European countries with firmly-based welfare states, the replacement rate (the ratio of unemployment and other benefits to post-tax income when previously

---

1 For a review of the relationship between the business cycle and poverty in Australia, Sweden, the United Kingdom and the United States, which takes account of labour market differences, see Pissarides (1991).

[72]

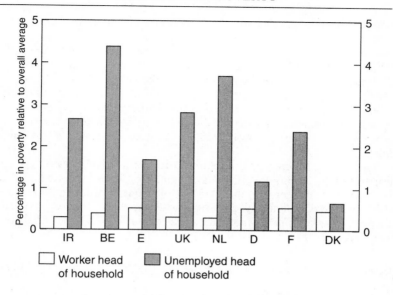

Figure 2.2 Poverty rate of workers and
unemployed: EU standard (expenditure basis).
Source: Hagenaars et al. (1994), tables A2.1.

employed) at its maximum is substantially less than 100 per cent. In
Germany, for instance, the benefit rate as a per centage of net earnings varies from 67 per cent for those with children and on unemployment insurance to 53 per cent for those without children and on
unemployment assistance (Missoc, 1996, p. 362). In the United Kingdom, the social transfer system, reliant on flat-rate benefits, cannot
be expected to offset fully for all of the unemployed the financial cost
of unemployment. Moreover, in a number of European countries,
the coverage of unemployment insurance and unemployment assistance is less than complete. Where the transfer is subject, for example,
to a family means-test, an unemployed person can receive no benefit
because his or her partner is earning above the means-test maximum.

The fact that transfers to the unemployed do not fully replace
earnings does not imply that unemployment leads to poverty. However, the results of Hagenaars et al. (1994) in figure 2.2 show that, in
a number of European countries in the late 1980s, the poverty rate
was much higher for households where the head was unemployed
than where the head was employed (in the non-agricultural sector).
In each case, the poverty rate is expressed relative to the overall rate
for the country. (Those countries are shown for which more than 3

per cent of households had a head recorded as unemployed.) In general, the poverty rate of workers is between a quarter and a half of the overall rate. In Denmark the poverty rate for the unemployed, while higher than for workers, is below the overall average; and in Germany it is only slightly above. On the other hand, in France, United Kingdom, Ireland, Netherlands and Belgium, the rate for the unemployed is more than twice that for workers. (This may of course reflect a low rate for workers, as in Belgium, but the absolute rate in Belgium for the unemployed is 28.9%, compared with 13.9% in Germany.)

The effect of increased unemployment on the poverty rate may be illustrated by a simple 'shift-share' analysis. If we assume for the moment that households only consist of single persons, who are either employed, unemployed or not-in-labour-force, then the contribution of workers and unemployed to the overall poverty rate, applying a poverty line π, is

$$G_w(\pi)N_w + G_u(\pi)N_u + G_n(\pi)N_n \tag{2.1}$$

where N_w, N_u, and N_n are the proportions of the population working, unemployed and not-in-labour-force, and $G_w(x)$, $G_u(x)$ and $G_n(x)$ are the proportions of workers, unemployed and not-in-labour-force with incomes (or expenditure) less than or equal to x. Suppose that ΔU workers, drawn randomly from the population of workers, become unemployed, with a distribution of income the same as that of the existing unemployed. The change in the overall poverty rate, for a given poverty line π, is

$$\Delta U[G_u(\pi) - G_w(\pi)] \tag{2.2}$$

Suppose that three-quarters of the population are in the labour force, then a difference in the poverty rate of 20 percentage points (as broadly in Belgium and France) would imply a 0.15 percentage point increase in the overall poverty rate for each 1 percentage point increase in the unemployment rate.[2] A difference of 40 percentage points, as in the United Kingdom, would imply an increase of 0.3 percentage points. On this basis, a rise in the unemployment rate of 5 percentage points, as in the European Union between the late 1970s and the early 1990s, could be expected to increase poverty by between 0.75 and 1.5 percentage points.

This simple shift-share analysis indicates a role for increased un-

---

2 This is calculated expressing ΔU as a per centage of the labour force (hence multiplying by 4/3).

employment which is important but smaller than the estimates for the United States. Moreover, there are certain respects in which this calculation may over-state the impact of increased unemployment. The assumptions about the characteristics of the newly unemployed may be unjustified; and the difference between the poverty rates over-stated. There are grounds for expecting them to be drawn dispro-portionately from the lower part of the distribution of workers and to be better off than the typical person already unemployed. These considerations reduce the expected impact on the poverty rate of a rise in unemployment. The rise in unemployment also reduces mean income, and hence reduces the poverty line where this is a proportion of mean income. Some people in the 'other category', for example, cease to be classified as poor even though as a group they are not affected, since they now appear to be better off relative to the mean.[3]

The decomposition is potentially misleading in that it treats indi-viduals on their own, rather than living in the families or households, which are the units of analysis when measuring poverty. An impor-tant part of the story is the number of earners per household. Figure 2.3 is again based on the results of Hagenaars et al. (1994), and shows the poverty rates in households with no earner, one earner, and two earners. Poverty rates are lower (except in Luxembourg) in two earner households. The difference between one- and two-earner households is, however, less (apart from Belgium) than that between one-earner and no-earner households. A change in the labour market which leads to x one-earner households becoming no-earner house-holds and x one earner households becoming two-earner households is neutral as far as total employment is concerned, but not necessarily neutral as far as poverty is concerned. In countries like the United Kingdom and Ireland, where the double difference is more than 20 percentage points[4], a shift of 5 per cent of households in each direc-tion would raise the poverty rate by 1 percentage point.

Moving from the individual unemployed person to the circum-stances of the household in which he or she lives may therefore pro-vide us with a different view of the impact of unemployment on poverty. At the same time, we see only imperfectly the allocation of resources within the household. The empirical estimates are based on

3 There is a good case for smoothing the poverty line so as to avoid cyclical variations of this type – see Atkinson et al. (1994, ch. 7).
4 In the United Kingdom, the poverty rate for no earner households is 38.1 per cent and that for one earner households 10.1 per cent, so the rise in poverty is 28.1 per centage points; the poverty rate for two earner house-holds is 3.0 per cent, so that the reduction from the switch from one to two earners is 7.1 per centage points. The difference between 28.1 and 7.1 is 21.0 percentage points.

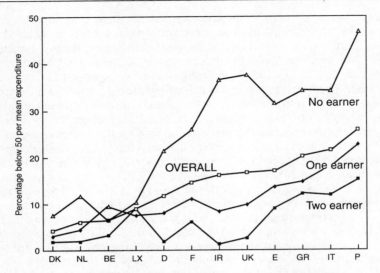

Figure 2.3 Poverty rates of households by number
of earners: European Community late 1980s.
Source: Hagenaars et al. (1994), tables A2.1.

the assumption that there is equal sharing, but this may not be the case. If the unemployed person does not share fully in the household resources, then the link between unemployment and poverty may be stronger.

The shift share decomposition focuses on the unemployed, whereas the US estimate took into account the impact on other groups, including the employed and the non-employed. There are other channels through which recession in the labour market increases poverty, and these are explored in the next section. On the other hand, we have seen in Lecture 1 that a number of the European Union countries have *not* experienced the rise in poverty of the magnitude which might be expected given the rise in unemployment. The evidence reviewed there showed for a number of European countries little overall rise in financial poverty since the 1970s. In figure 2.4, the diamonds show the actual percentage point increases in poverty rates, from the late 1970s to the early 1990s, for eight European Union countries (those shown in figures 1.13 and 1.14 with the exception of Belgium, where the series only starts in 1985). If the percentage point increase had been in line with that in unemployment (between 1974–9 and 1990–3), as with the Blank-Blinder pre-1983 results, then the points would have been on the dashed line. If we take into account the fall in inflation

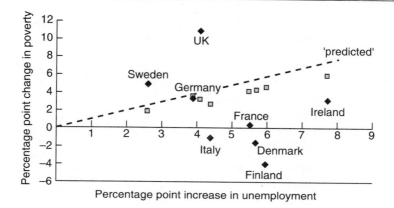

Figure 2.4 Changes in poverty and increases in
unemployment in Europe: late 1970s to early 1990s.
Sources: changes in poverty see figures 1.13 and 1.14, change
in unemployment (1974–9) to (1990–3) for total labour force
from OECD (1995), table 2.15.

between 1973–9 and 1989–93 (*OECD*, 1995, table 8.11), subtract-
ing a seventh of this amount, then we get the 'predicted' squares.
(The multiplication by one-seventh is again based on the estimates
of Blank and Blinder.) Both the UK and Sweden have larger increases in poverty than expected; Germany is very close to the
prediction; and all the other five countries have a much smaller
increase in poverty than expected, including four with no increase
(or a fall).

Does this mean that we need not be concerned about unemployment in Europe? There is a risk, as recently emphasized by Amartya
Sen (1997), that Europeans become complacent about their levels of
unemployment. He contrasts attitudes in the United States and Europe:

> American social ethics finds it possible to be very non-supportive of
> the indigent and the impoverished, in a way that the typical West
> European, reared in a welfare state, finds hard to accept. But the same
> American social ethics would find the double-digit levels of unemploy-
> ment, common in Europe, to be quite intolerable. (1997, p. 9)

If, as Sen urges, we are to combine the successful features of both
approaches, then we need to look more fully at the causes of unemployment.

[77]

2.2 Economics of Unemployment and Exclusion in the Labour Market

In his survey of European unemployment, Bean concludes that 'there does not seem to be any single cause of the rise in European unemployment'. He goes on to say that:

> The European experience points to the possibility of both a much richer set of determinants of the equilibrium unemployment rate and the existence of important persistence mechanisms that do not appear in the standard model. (Bean, 1994, p. 615)

A wide variety of theories have indeed been advanced. Lindbeck (1993), for example, lists the following possible micro-economic explanations: government controls (minimum wage legislation), social norms against under-bidding of wages, trade unions, efficiency wages, and insider/outsider theories.

There are nonetheless common features to a number of the theories. According to Lindbeck, we can: 'postulate a typical wage setting function for this set of theories' (1993, p. 56), where the wage-setting curve is such that the real wage, w, rises with the ratio of total employment to total available labour supply (taken as fixed) – see figure 2.5. This is combined with aggregate labour demand, which is a declining function of the real wage. The resulting level of employment, and hence unemployment, is shown in figure 2.5.

While this aggregate labour market formulation provides an overall structure, the policy implications depend on what lies behind the wage-setting curve. Suppose, for example, that the wage setting curve is based on union wage determination. To introduce trade unions into the picture, we have to make assumptions about the membership that they represent, the objectives which they pursue, and the nature of the bargaining process. None of these is straight forward. Here I simply investigate the implications of one set of assumptions (for further discussion, see Layard et al., 1991, ch. 2; and Booth, 1995). Wages are bargained between a union and firms in an industry in the knowledge that firms will choose their employment in the light of the negotiated wage (it is a 'right to manage' theory of bargaining, rather than an 'efficient bargain'). The outcome of bargaining is to maximize the product of profits and the excess of the wage bill over the value of the workers' outside option (denoted by z), raised to a power which reflects the bargaining strength of the union. This leads to a wage w_i for union i which is related to the value of the outside option by

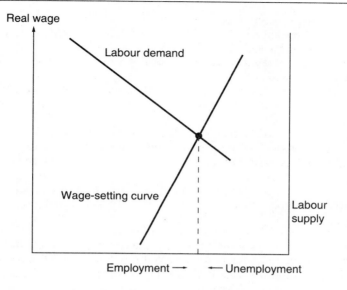

Figure 2.5 Labour market equilibrium with unemployment.

$w_i/(w_i-z) =$ elasticity of labour demand

                         +

                         relative employer/union ratio of bargaining power to cost share

          $\equiv$ ξ (2.3)

The wage is closer to z, the larger is the elasticity of labour demand (which is a derived demand and depends on the product market conditions), and the greater the relative bargaining power of the employers (compared with the shares in value added). If the alternative open to workers not employed in the sector for which the union negotiates is to work elsewhere with probability $(1-u)$, or to receive benefit, b, with probability u,[5] and all sectors are identical (so that the wage elsewhere is equal to w_i), then the resulting aggregate wage-setting curve is given by

$$w = b / [1 - 1/(u\xi)] \qquad (2.4)$$

5 Here it is simply assumed that the unemployed automatically receive benefit; this assumption is debatable – see Atkinson and Micklewright (1991).

so that the location of the wage-setting curve depends on the benefit level, the elasticity of demand, and the relative bargaining power (compared to cost share).

From this expression, combined with the labour demand curve, we can see that policy measures on the supply side can reduce unemployment. Two classes of measures stand out. Legislative and other changes can reduce the bargaining power of trade unions, and hence the bargained wage. Cuts in unemployment benefit again reduce wage demands, and reduce unemployment. These measures may be seen as an 'Anglo-Saxon' solution to unemployment, and contrasted with the Continental desire to retain social partnership and preserve social protection.

What can we deduce for the relationship with poverty? The cut in benefit is double-edged. It reduces the proportion unemployed, but at the expense of lowering the incomes of those unemployed. On the other hand, we would expect to see a fall in poverty from the reduction in union bargaining power, on the assumption that the union wage is above the poverty line. Such a move towards labour market flexibility would redistribute from the 'privileged' union members to the 'excluded' unemployed. If this model were an accurate account of the way in which labour markets operate, then social exclusion may be seen as arising from the actions of the trade unions. The unwillingness of European governments to adopt Anglo-Saxon labour flexibility policies is, from this perspective, responsible for the persistence of unemployment.

It is not my intention here to debate the relationship between labour market flexibility and unemployment (which I have discussed in Atkinson, forthcoming). I do, however, want to take issue with the proposition that the adoption of Anglo-Saxon measures, by reducing unemployment, will necessarily reduce poverty and social exclusion. For this purpose, the model outlined above is seriously incomplete. In particular, the aggregate labour market model takes no account of differences among the employed. Even if, on average, wages are above the poverty line, this is not true of all workers. There are the working poor. A move towards greater labour market flexibility may worsen the position of the low paid, increasing the poverty rate among the employed. The assumption of homogeneous workers means that the models do not lend themselves to the identification of groups of *workers* who may be socially excluded.

The importance of considering the distribution among workers is brought out by the study of the United States by Blank (1993), in which she revisits the relationship between poverty rates and unemployment estimated by Blank and Blinder (1986) over the period 1959–83. From 1983 to 1989 the United States saw a period of expansion, with unemployment falling from 9.5 per cent to 5.2 per cent (OECD, 1995, table 2.15). The experience of such an expansion is of especial interest to Europe today, but the record as far as poverty is concerned is not encouraging. The relationship estimated earlier by Blank and Blinder would have predicted a fall in the poverty rate from 15.2 per cent in 1983 to 9.3 per cent in 1989, but in fact the fall was only to 12.8 per cent. (In considering these findings, it should be borne in mind that the poverty line was adjusted over time in line with the Consumer Price Index.) The reason is to be found, according to Blank, in a change in the responsiveness to macro-economic conditions of the earnings of the poor. Whereas in the 1960s expansion the poor benefited from rising weekly wages, in the 1980s their real wages declined. As has been widely documented, there has been a widening of the earnings distribution.

Models of unemployment with differences between workers

The customary economic models do not embody the structure necessary to draw direct conclusions about poverty and social exclusion, since they do not allow for differences among the employed or among the unemployed. In what follows, I seek to allow for one of these elements: differences between people in potential productivity. Although this is only one of the dimensions along which people differ, it takes us a step closer to reality.

It is now assumed that there is a distribution of people with productivity n, where n is greater than or equal to a strictly positive n_{min}, and the proportion with productivity less than or equal to n is denoted by the cumulative distribution function $G(n)$, with associated density function $g(n)$. (Readers may feel that this is over-heavy use of mathematical notation, but it is unfortunately the case that the model becomes more complicated once we allow for differences between people.) A worker is either employed, contributing n to labour input and earning a wage $w(n)$, or not employed, producing domestic output $k(n)$, and receiving a benefit, $b(n)$. A worker of type n is assumed to prefer to work where

$$w(n) > \theta[k(n) + b(n)] \tag{2.5}$$

The form of the benefit allows for flat-rate benefits as in the United Kingdom or for earnings-related benefits as in Continental European countries. The parameter ι may be greater than 1 where people require a premium over the value of home production (plus benefit) or may be less than 1 if, other things equal, they prefer employment.

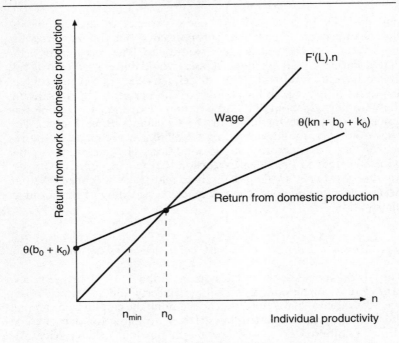

Figure 2.6 Competitive labour market with different labour productivities.

Employers produce a single output. They are assumed to maximize profit, taking the output price as given (it is taken as the numeraire: i.e. wages are valued in terms of output). Output is a function, $F(L)$, of the total labour employed, L, where F is an increasing strictly concave function. The inputs of workers are perfect substitutes in the sense that total labour is the integral of $nL(n)$, where $L(n)$ is the amount of labour of type n employed. (This is the model employed by Mirrlees, 1971, in his treatment of the optimum income tax.)

The first case considered is that of a perfectly competitive labour market, where firms and workers treat $w(n)$ as outside their influence. The return per unit of labour is $F'[L]$, and a worker of type n receives a wage $nF'[L]$. Figure 2.6 illustrates the determination of the equilibrium in the case where domestic output is $(kn + k_o)$, where k and k_o are positive constants, and there is a flat-rate benefit (b_o). Firms employ all workers with n larger than a value n_o; from (2.5) they are willing to work at that wage, and there is an equilibrium provided that

$$L = \int_{n_0}^{\infty} n \, g(n) \, dn \tag{2.6}$$

which is the total work capacity above n_0.

There are two types of equilibrium. One is where the marginal product of labour when all workers are employed is sufficiently large that firms can pay the least productive worker in excess of his or her reservation wage. There is then full employment. The second type of equilibrium has less than full employment in the market, as is shown in figure 2.6, where workers with productivity between n_{min} and n_0 are not employed. The extent of market employment depends on several factors. One is the level of productivity in the market as opposed to productivity at home. A 'shock' to overall productivity, reducing $F'(L)$ at every L, raises n_0 and hence reduces market employment. The extent of market employment depends also on the level of unemployment benefit, and on the relative valuation of market and other income.

This framework yields some of the same conclusions as the aggregate labour market model with identical workers. A cut in the benefit level increases market employment. On the other hand, we can now address the issue of poverty wages. If the benefit is set at a flat rate which is below the poverty line, and the unemployed set a low value on benefit income and home production, then people take jobs paying less than the poverty line, and cuts in benefit increase the number of the employed who are in financial poverty. On the other hand, in a world described by this model, it can be said that the existence of unemployment benefit makes it more likely that low productivity workers will choose to exclude themselves from market employment. There is possibly a contradictory relationship between avoidance of poverty and avoidance of social exclusion. The welfare state has been criticized as creating 'benefit dependency'. The extent of such exclusion depends on individual behaviour, here embodied in the parameter θ, and this in turn may be influenced by social norms. A high valuation of independence by society as a whole may lead people to choose to work even where there is no financial gain. At the same time, such norms may be endogenous. Lindbeck (1995) has argued, for example that where the proportion of recipients exceeds some critical mass, adherence to previously accepted norms may be progressively diminished, leading to 'hazardous Welfare State dynamics'.

The risk of exclusion depends on the structure of benefits. This applies both to the balance between fixed rate and proportional elements in the benefit formula, and to the conditionality of benefits. The payment of a basic income irrespective of employment status, for instance, would be neutral with respect to the work choice set out above. Such a universal benefit would be inclusionary rather than exclusionary. On the other hand, if the basic income is financed by a tax on market work, then this will reduce employment more than the tax necessary to finance the unemployment benefit, since the budgetary cost is higher.

A different form of government intervention is via a minimum wage. Suppose that this is set by the government at the poverty level, and that this is above the level of wages which clears the market in figure 2.6 (which can only be the case where the effective level of benefit (θb_o) is below the poverty line). The minimum wage would reduce the level of market employment and raise the wage per unit of labour input. In this competitive labour market model, a minimum wage set at the poverty line means that there is a group of people who are both in poverty and excluded from the labour market. On the other hand, in the absence of the minimum wage they would be working for a wage below the poverty line. The abolition of the minimum wage would end social exclusion but not poverty.[6]

One lesson from this model of differences between workers is that the extent of exclusion depends not just on the lack of skills of those with low productivity, but on the whole distribution of abilities. Suppose, for example, that people in the upper part of the skill distribution become more productive. There is then an increase in the total labour supplied and a fall in F' at any value of n_o, so that the equilibrium exclusion point rises. Less productive workers are valued less because others have become more productive. This is an example of interdependence, where the poor are affected by what happens to other, more fortunate groups, a theme which recurs in this Lecture. The conclusion would be moderated if their labour inputs were less than perfect substitutes, but we have also to consider the interrelation with other factors of production, notably capital. The demand for less skilled labour may be differentially affected by changes in the real rate of return, or by technological change.

Suppose now that we consider a different pattern of operation for the labour market. Workers and jobs are matched on a one-to-one basis. Jobs are on offer to workers with specified productivity. (An employer can immediately judge the productivity of a worker.) If jobs are offered to people of type n, then it is assumed that at all dates all such workers have a job offer. A job match creates a 'surplus' of output over the reservation wage:

6 This analysis is predicated on a competitive labour market. The same conclusions do not necessarily carry over to other models of the labour market, particularly where the employer has monopsony power (see, for example, Dickens et al., 1994) or where there is investment in human capital.

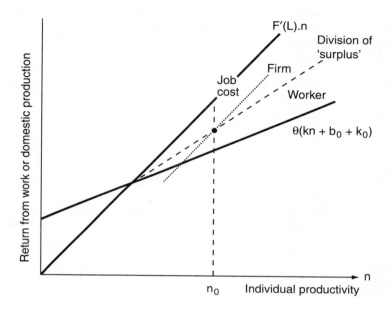

Figure 2.7 Job creation, bargaining, and
unemployment.

$$F'(L)n - \theta\{k(n) + b(n)\} \tag{2.7}$$

A process of bilateral negotiation leads to a worker and his or her
employer sharing the 'surplus' in proportions γ and $(1-\gamma)$, so that the
wage is

$$w(n) = \gamma \, F'(L)n + (1-\gamma) \, \theta\{k(n) + b(n)\}] \tag{2.8}$$

There is assumed to be a fixed cost of creating a job vacancy, c, a
sunk cost when it comes to the negotiation, so that employers create
jobs only where their share of the surplus exceeds this fixed cost:

$$(1-\gamma)[F'(L)n - \theta\{k(n) + b(n)\}] \geq c \tag{2.9}$$

If free entry drives the value of a job down to c, then the resulting
equilibrium is shown in figure 2.7, which is drawn on the assumption
of a flat-rate benefit, b_o, and that productivity in home production is
linear in n (as in figure 2.6). The point n_o is such that the surplus to

[85]

the firm, measured down from $F'(L)n$, is equal to c. This where the dotted line (surplus equal to c) cuts the dashed line (bargained division of the surplus).

The proportion of the population who receive no job offers depends on the same factors as before: productivity in the market as opposed to productivity at home, on the level and structure of unemployment benefit, and on the relative valuation of market and other income. But it also depends on the relative bargaining power of workers and employers, and on the cost of job creation. The larger the share of the surplus that goes to workers, the higher unemployment. However, even if workers are willing to work for only their reservation wage, the existence of the cost of job creation creates a barrier to their employment which they are powerless to overcome.

The possibility that workers may not be able to 'price themselves' into the labour market has received prominence in 'efficiency wage' theories of unemployment. There are several reasons why firms may refuse to take on workers at a lower wage; here I simply take one as an illustration. Suppose that the job matches described in the previous paragraphs continue over time, with no further set-up cost, but there is a probability δ that they will terminate at any given date. This probability depends on the wage in that workers with a higher surplus over their reservation wage are less likely to quit:

$$\delta[w(n) - \theta\{k(n) + b(n)\}] \tag{2.10}$$

where $\delta()$ is a decreasing function.

The firm may then pay a higher wage $w(n)$ to people of type n in order to reduce turnover (see, for example, Weiss, 1990, p 59). Discounting at rate r, the expected value of a job of type n to the employer is

$$V = [F'(L)n - w(n)] / (r + \delta) \tag{2.11}$$

The first point to be noted is that if free entry requires that the present value of a job, V, equals c, then the impact of this condition depends on the rate of discount applied by employers. A rise in r, either because real interest rates have risen, or because employers are requiring a shorter payback period, raises the hurdle and causes more workers to be unemployed. A person of low skill may be excluded from a job on account of employers adopting a more short-term horizon: they are not willing to invest in job creation. In terms of figure 2.7, the dotted line moves down, leading to a rise in n_o (the effect on the full equilibrium has, of course, to allow for the effect on L).

Where turnover varies with the wage, the profit maximizing choice of $w(n)$ for a given n may be shown to be (where δ' is increasing)

$$-\delta'[w(n) - \theta\{k(n) + b(n)\}] = 1/c \qquad (2.12)$$

The firm sets the wage above the reservation wage by an amount which, with the specific assumptions made, is constant. A worker may offer to work for less, but it is not profitable for the employer to accept the offer, since the worker is more likely to quit. We may then have a situation where there is a 'rigid' wage for less productive workers, set by efficiency wage considerations, but where the wages of more productive workers are set by bargaining, and hence affected by, for instance, shocks to aggregate productivity. The more productive workers face risks concerning their wage level; the less productive are exposed to variations in employment.

Conclusion

Avoidance of poverty does not imply social inclusion, in that people may be above the poverty line but excluded from jobs. This could happen if the state provides a flat-rate unemployment benefit sufficient to reach the poverty line. Conversely, if benefits are set low or abolished, then workers may be in the labour force, and in this sense socially included, but they may be earning poverty wages. Inclusion does not guarantee escape from poverty. Moreover, people may leave the formal economy and depend solely on home production. In this latter case, we have potentially both exclusion and poverty.

The economic models reviewed in this section do not in themselves provide full explanations of European unemployment, but they do serve to bring out some important considerations. We have seen that the position of the low skilled is influenced by the circumstances of the more advantaged. We cannot consider the unemployed or low paid in isolation from the better off. Increasing skill advantage of those higher up the scale can have adverse effects at the bottom. There are several different processes by which people may be excluded from the labour market. It may be the benefit system itself; it may be the consequence of trade union monopoly power; or it may reflect the short payback period demanded by firms and their reluctance to create new jobs. The last of these should be stressed, since too little attention is paid in public discussion to the role of employers in job creation and the way in which changes in the capital market have rebounded on the labour market.

In this section, exclusion has been equated with unemployment, but it is not the only dimension of social seclusion, and I turn now to exclusion in consumption.

[87]

2.3 Pricing of Goods and Exclusion from the Market

An important strand in the concerns expressed about social exclusion is that people are unable to participate in the customary consumption activities of the society in which they live. The most evident example is that of housing, in the extreme case homelessness, but also significant are access to durables, food expenditure (nutritional content), and expenditure relating to recreational, cultural and leisure activities (Ramprakash, 1994). The last of these is particularly relevant to families with children. Peer-group pressure may mean that a Manchester United shirt or Nike trainers are necessary for children to be included in neighbourhood activities. Exclusion may apply not just to goods but also to services. The poor may be excluded from insurance cover where premia are set on a postcode basis; banks may refuse on similar criteria to open bank accounts or to issue credit cards.

A good example of exclusion in consumption is the telephone. A person unable to afford a telephone finds it difficult to participate in a society where the majority have telephones. Children are not invited out to play, because neighbours no longer call round – they call up. Letters do not allow the same contact to be kept with relatives who have moved away. A person applying for a job may not be called for interview since he or she cannot be contacted directly. This may sound like an advertisement for the telephone companies, but it is on them – and other suppliers of key goods and services – that I would like now to focus attention. The conditions under which goods are supplied is an aspect which is overlooked in the analysis of poverty. The pricing decisions of the suppliers determine whether or not the poor are excluded from this dimension of consumption.[7]

To begin with, let us assume that the good in question is indivisible.[8] Households consume either one unit of the good or none, and it is possible, by assumption, to survive physically without the good. A household either has a telephone or not, and can physically survive without one, even if they are precluded from participation in social activities. Let us also suppose that there is a single profit-maximizing monopolist supplying the good. If a household pays a price p for the good in question, and has income m, then it has $(m-p)$

7 I am drawing here on the work of Jean Gabszewicz and Jacques Thisse (for example, 1979) and Avner Shaked and John Sutton (for example, 1982). See also Gabszewicz, Shaked, Sutton and Thisse (1986).
8 Lewis and Ulph (1988) examine the implications of there being a strictly positive quantity of certain goods required to avoid poverty, although they do not investigate the conditions under which these goods are supplied.

available for other consumption. Assume that the utility derived from consumption, when the good is bought, is given simply by

$$U = (1 + x) (m-p) \qquad (2.13)$$

where x denotes the advantage over not purchasing the good, so that utility in the latter case is given simply by $U = m$. The household decides to purchase the good if $U \geq m$, or if

$$p \leq x/(1 + x). \, m \equiv \mu \, m \qquad (2.14)$$

The household is priced out of the market if the price is set at too high a fraction of its income.

To make this concrete, suppose that there are two groups in work, one receiving a high wage w_{max} and the other receiving a low wage w_{min}, and a third group on benefits, b, assumed to be below w_{min}. The monopolist may sell to all three groups, in which case he charges a price of μb. Or he may decide to get a higher price, even at the expense of excluding those on benefit, charging either μw_{min} and selling it to both wage-earning groups, or μw_{max} and selling to only the higher paid. The choice between these will depend on the number of people in each of the groups and on the relation between their incomes. People in the lowest income group – those on benefits – are excluded from the market if their income falls too low relative to that of those in work. The level of benefit needed to avoid exclusion depends on the position of others in the society: the wages and the number of workers in the lower skill group. In this way, we have made a – perhaps unexpected – connection between the theory of imperfect competition and the idea of exclusion which one finds in the poverty literature.

The model of an indivisible demand is examined further in the next section; before that I consider the case closer to textbook demand theory where the quantity consumed, x, is a variable, as with the number of telephone calls or electricity consumption.

Utility prices and two-part tariffs

A household can survive without making a purchase, a situation which we represent again by $x = 0$, or it can buy a quantity x, in which case it pays a price p per unit plus T, a fixed charge.[9] In other

9 The charge is discussed in terms of a standing charge, payable on a recurrent basis, but there may also be connection charges, payable on a once-off basis.

words, there is a two-part tariff. The utility derived from consumption, when the household subscribes, is now given by

$$U = (1 + x) (m-px-T) \tag{2.15}$$

The level of x consumed is that which maximizes U: i.e.

$$x = (m-T-p)/2p \tag{2.16}$$

and the resulting level of utility is

$$V = (m-T+p)^2/4p \tag{2.17}$$

The household decides to subscribe if V is greater than m: i.e.

$$m \geq p + T + 2 \sqrt{(pT)} \equiv m_o \tag{2.18}$$

which determines the critical value, m_o, at which a household is indifferent for any given p and T, where (2.18) holds with equality. Households with income below m_o are excluded from the market.

The optimal choice of a two-part tariff by a profit-maximizing enterprise has been discussed by Walter Oi:

> If you were owner of Disneyland, should you charge high lump sum admission fees and give the rides away, or should you let people into the amusement park for nothing and stick them with high monopolistic prices for the rides? (1971, p 77)

He goes on to show that if the monopolist is legally compelled to charge the same admission fee and price per ride to all customers (in other words, it cannot be a discriminating monopoly), then it is quite possible that the profit-maximizing price excludes some customers from the market.

This analysis is especially relevant where the supply of the good or service has passed from public to private hands. Whereas it would be open to the government to require *public* enterprises to choose p and T such that m_o is no higher than the lowest level of income (for example, that households living on social assistance can afford electricity), privatization requires that some mechanism be put in place to avoid exclusion of low-income customers, since this may well be profitable for the new management. Where the industry is regulated, then an access condition can be imposed by the regulators. In the case of telephones in the United States:

> 'Universal Access' has been a historical commitment of the telecommunications industry and its regulators. (Gillis et al., 1986, p 35)

The United Kingdom privatization legislation contains an obligation to supply 'all reasonable demands', but this is open to a variety of interpretations. According to Burns et al.:

> the social provisions put upon the privatized utilities were pretty minimal. (1995, p. 17)

As they note:

> the political mood at the time of the major privatisations saw the industries as wealth creators, not instruments of social policy. (1995, p. 17)

There has been considerable anxiety about the impact of new tariff structures on poor households. For example, Hancock and Price (1995) have studied the new gas tariffs, identifying a form of multiple exclusion, whereby consumers who do not have access to bank accounts cannot benefit from the cheaper prices available to those who pay by direct debit.

Where no universal access condition is imposed by the regulators, then the impact of private profit-maximizing firms depends on the degree of competition. If a monopolist prices in such a way as to exclude the poorest consumers from the market, would it be profitable for new entrants to come into the market? This clearly depends on the cost of entry, where competition policy plays a role. In this respect, we are making a connection between two different spheres of government policy.

What account should be taken of these distributional concerns in the design of regulation and competition policy? This question has not received a great deal of attention – in contrast to the literature on the distributional dimensions of pricing when utilities are state owned. Where it is discussed, the view appears to be that regulators should not take account of equity objectives, and achievement of redistribution should be confined to the tax and social security systems. In part, this argument is made on welfare economic grounds:

> any attempt to redistribute through regulation will typically be just as costly in economic terms as redistribution by taxes and benefits, and almost certainly more costly. (Burns et al., 1995, p. 17)

It is, however, a matter of comparing two sets of costs. There is no a priori reason to suppose that the welfare-maximizing policy involves no adjustment to the pricing and other policies of utility companies. In part, the argument runs on public choice lines:

the advantages of regulators having discretion to pursue distributional ends are outweighed by disadvantages of capture, influence activities, uncertainty, and unaccountability. (Vickers, 1997, p. 18)

Again this requires a comparison of the costs on both sides. Redistribution through the tax and benefit system is also subject to political pressures.

If privatization leads to poor consumers facing higher prices, the increased price should in theory enter the price index used to adjust the poverty line. However, the price index may not fully reflect the budget patterns of the poor (for example, a larger share spent on energy). The index may not capture the burden of the fixed charge element for small consumers, nor other ways in which costs are higher: for example where the supplier insists on pre-payment meters. There is, moreover, a second way in which the poor may be affected by decisions on the supply side and which may not be captured in a price index: via the range of quantities and qualities available in the shops. I turn now to this aspect.

2.4 Exclusion, Rising Living Standards and the Availability of Products

People may be excluded from the market not just by price but because the goods they would choose to buy are simply no longer available. There are limitations on the range of goods which are available. A list of necessary goods drawn up a century ago would probably have included paraffin lamps, which, if available today, are certainly hard to find (ships' chandlers do still stock them – I recently bought some for my traditional sailing boat!). Availability is a question of access, and here we come again to the decisions of suppliers, which have transformed many aspects of our lives in recent years. As has been noted in the case of food:

Recent decades have seen dramatic changes in food retailing . . . there are more out-of-town superstores and fewer small shops. In general, this trend has been beneficial . . . Some consumers, however, are unable to take advantage of these developments and have been left behind. (Piachaud and Webb, 1996, p. 2)

The poor are disproportionately affected:

access to healthy diets [is] a particular problem for low income households . . . while some low income areas are not totally deprived of a supermarket or other large grocery store, the choice of retailer or store

[92]

format may be extremely limited. (Low Income Project Team, 1996, pp. 6–7)

In order to explore this further, I return to the case of the consumption of an indivisible good. I assume that in order to go to work in the labour market a person requires, in addition to time, the input of a specified, indivisible commodity.[10] The person consumes only a single unit of this commodity, which costs p. All other goods are aggregated into a numeraire. Without the capacity to travel to work, the person can only work domestically earning a wage n, which is lower than the wage, $(\lambda + 1)n$, obtainable in the labour market. (The reader will note the parallel with the model of section 2.2.) The viability of work in the labour market requires that

$$\lambda n \geq p \qquad (2.19)$$

People differ in their values of n, which is an index of productivity, and hence of how well-off they are (there is assumed to be no other form of income). There is again a cumulative distribution function, $G(n)$, with associated density function, $g(n)$. The density is zero for all values of n below n_{min}, where n_{min} is strictly positive. Of particular interest is the proportion of people 'excluded' from participation in the labour market, $G(n_o)$, where n_o is such that (2.19) holds with equality.

The commodity is produced at a constant marginal cost, c, per unit. If there are no fixed costs, and the industry is perfectly competitive, then the price charged is c, and all are capable of participating in the labour market where

$$n_{min} \geq c / \lambda \qquad (2.20)$$

It is assumed in what follows that this condition is satisfied: the lowest wage is always sufficient to induce participation where the good is priced at marginal cost.

Suppose now that, in addition to the constant variable cost, there is also a fixed cost of production, C, and that in these conditions the good is supplied by a single monopolist who sets a price p to maximize profit. Since each person buys only one unit, total sales are

$$1 - G(p/\lambda) \quad \text{where } n_o \geq n_{min} \qquad (2.21a)$$

$$1 \quad \text{where } n_o < n_{min} \qquad (2.21b)$$

10 The analysis follows that in Atkinson, 1995a, which contains further details.

[93]

Where (2.21a) holds, the level of profit, P, is given by

$$P = (p - c)(1 - G(p/\lambda)) - C \tag{2.22}$$

The derivative with respect to price is

$$\partial P/\partial p = 1 - G(n_o) - (p - c) g(n_o) n_o / p \tag{2.23}$$

It is evident that the monopolist will not charge a price below λn_{min}, since to do so would reduce revenue on existing sales without adding to total sales (since at that price all households would be buying the good). Evaluating the derivative (2.23) at this lowest price, we can see that it is profitable to the monopolist to raise the price above this level, and hence exclude certain people from the market, where

$$g(n_{min}) [n_{min} - c/\lambda] < 1 \tag{2.24}$$

Given the assumption that condition (2.20) holds, that is everyone buys the good if it is priced at marginal cost, the square bracket is positive, and the monopolist does not exclude customers providing the initial density is sufficiently large. However, if the initial density is sufficiently small, then there is a profit-maximizing interior solution where[11]

$$(p - c)/p = ([1 - G(n_o)] / [n_o g(n_o)]) \tag{2.25}$$

Whether or not the monopolist sets the price to exclude the lowest productivity people depends on the overall distribution. This may be illustrated by two special cases. Suppose first that there is a *uniform* distribution between n_{min} and n_{max}, with density $1/ [n_{max} - n_{min}]$. The condition (2.24) then becomes

$$n_{min} \geq \tfrac{1}{2} [n_{max} + c/\lambda] \tag{2.26}$$

It follows that, if the productivity of the least able per-son is less than half that of the most able, then some customers are excluded by the

11 The second-order condition is satisfied at this turning point where

$$(1-G)g'/g2 + 2 \geq 0$$

A non-decreasing hazard rate $(g/(1-G))$ is sufficient but not necessary. The second-order condition is satisfied for both of the special distributions considered below.

monopoly pricing.[12] In this case the profit-maximizing price is given by

$$p = \frac{1}{2} [c + \lambda\, n_{\max}] \tag{2.27}$$

In other words, it is the average of the marginal cost and the maximum that anyone is willing to pay. The value of n at which people are excluded is

$$n_o = \frac{1}{2} [n_{\max} + c/\lambda] \tag{2.28}$$

A second example is provided by the *Pareto* distribution, where for n greater than or equal to $n_{\min}$

$$1 - G(n) = (n/n_{\min})^{-a} \tag{2.29}$$

where · is greater than 1. The condition (2.24) then becomes

$$a\, [1 - c\, /\, (\lambda n_{\min})] < 1 \tag{2.30}$$

If the marginal cost is, say, three-quarters of the willingness to pay of the least able, this is satisfied where · is less than 4. Where condition (2.30) is satisfied, the profit-maximizing price involves a mark-up

$$(p - c)/p = 1\, /\, a \tag{2.31}$$

With a equal to 4, the price is 4/3 times the marginal cost. The value of n at which people are excluded is

$$n_o = a/(a-1) \cdot (c/\lambda) \tag{2.32}$$

Rising living standards and inequality

What is the effect, in this simple model, of a general rise in living standards? Suppose that there is an equal proportional rise in n for everyone, increasing the purchasing power of wages in terms of the numéraire commodity. The cost of production, c, is unchanged. At any given p a larger proportion of the population can afford the

12 Readers familiar with the work of Shaked and Sutton (1982) will recognize my debt to their model. The assumption made about preferences is, however, different here, being the same as that in Tirole (1989, p. 296), although in this latter case the differences between consumers are in a taste parameter rather than in their endowment.

product. However, does the monopolist react by raising the price?

The answer depends on the form of the distribution, as is demonstrated by the two special examples. With a Pareto distribution, if condition (2.31) applies, the price is a constant multiple of the marginal cost and hence is unchanged. The income necessary to avoid exclusion is unchanged as living standards rise, and a larger proportion can indeed afford the product. On the other hand, with the uniform distribution, the necessary income rises, as may be seen from (2.26) where n_{max} increases. The increase is, however, less than proportional, and the proportion of the population excluded falls, as may be seen from the fact that in the case of the uniform distribution

$$G(n_o) = 1 - \frac{1}{2} \left[n_{max} - c/\lambda\right] / \left[n_{max} - n_{min}\right] \tag{2.33}$$

If a rise in the average income is accompanied by widening inequality, then the outcome may be different. Suppose that, in the case of the uniform distribution, there is a rise in n_{max}, holding n_{min} constant, so that the distribution becomes more thinly spread. From (2.33) it may be seen that the proportion excluded from the market rises towards a half. Where the exclusion of customers was not previously profitable, it may become so, as may be seen from (2.24), since $g(n_{min})$ is reduced and the square bracket unchanged. In the case of the Pareto distribution, a fall in · has the effect of reducing the density at n_{min} and of increasing the density at the upper tail. Again it becomes more likely that people with low values of n are excluded. A fall in a from 4 to 3 has the effect of increasing the monopoly mark-up over marginal cost from 33⅓ per cent to 50 per cent.

These results show once more how the implications of possessing a specified level of productivity, n, depend on the distribution of productivities elsewhere in society. A person in one society may have the capacity to take part in the labour market, but in another be excluded because the existence of people with higher productivities leads the monopoly supplier to price the good out of his or her reach. Depending on the form of the distribution, rising living standards may increase the income necessary to ensure the specified capacity, and this is accentuated by rising inequality.

Choice of quality

Economic growth may not only raise average incomes; it may also bring new products. The range of goods which could potentially contribute to the activity of 'working' may be extended. A person may be able to choose between a bicycle and a higher quality alternative, such as a motor-cycle, as a means of getting to work. The higher quality alternative may allow the person to achieve a higher wage, because he or she can work longer hours, or put in greater effort, or travel further afield, etc. The availability of this choice does however depend on the range of goods supplied.

Suppose that the model is extended to allow the monopolist a choice over the quality, λ, of the good supplied, where λ varies between λ_{min} and λ_{max}, with associated (constant) marginal cost $c(\lambda)$ and fixed cost $C(\lambda)$. It is assumed initially that he supplies only one quality. Suppose that, at the lowest quality, the profit-maximizing price is such as to exclude part of the population. Does the availability of superior qualities lead the proportion excluded to rise or fall?

The effect on the choice of quality by the monopolist may be seen by differentiating profit (equation (2.22)) with respect to λ, and making use of the condition (2.25) for the choice of price (at the lowest quality we have an interior solution)

$$\partial P/\partial \lambda = [1 - G(n_o)] (n_o - \partial c/\partial \lambda) - \partial C/\partial \lambda \qquad (2.34)$$

Whether or not this is positive depends on how the costs of production change as we move to goods of higher quality. Similarly from the condition (2.25) for the profit-maximising choice of price,

$$(1 - G(n_o) - (n_o - c/\lambda) g(n_o) = 0 \qquad (2.35)$$

(where the second-order conditions require the left hand side to be a declining function of n_o), we can deduce that whether or not n_o increases with λ depends on how c/λ changes. If c/λ rises, then n_o rises.

Various situations may be imagined with regard to the variation of costs with quality. Shaked and Sutton (1983) note that quality improvements may involve largely research and development costs, in which case the marginal production costs may rise only slowly with increases in quality. Suppose that the effective cost per quality unit, c/λ, falls with λ, so that $\partial c/\partial \lambda$ is less than c/λ. Since by assumption the initial value of c/λ is no greater than n_{min}, and hence no greater than the initial n_o, it follows that the monopolist prefers to increase quality unless there is too large an increase in fixed cost.[13] If this holds over the whole range of possible λ, then the monopolist chooses the highest quality λ_{max}. The production of a superior product does not, however, exclude poorer consumers, since the reduced cost per unit of quality (c/λ) is passed on, at least in part, to consumers and n_o falls. The

---

13 There is clearly a difference between fixed costs which are once-for-all, like initial research and development, and those which arise each production period; C refers to the latter.

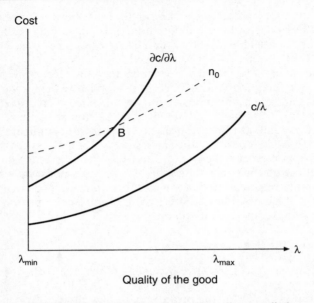

Figure 2.8 Monopolist choice of quality supplied.

greater effectiveness of motor-cycles more than outweighs the higher price.

A different situation is that where there are diminishing returns to quality production, in that the effective cost c/λ rises with λ, and $\partial c/\partial\lambda$ is greater than c/λ. The fact that n_o is then initially above c/λ, by assumption, is not then sufficient to ensure that the first term in (2.34) is positive. It is therefore possible that the monopolist remains content with the lowest quality. On the other hand, it is also possible that an increase in quality is profitable, providing that fixed costs do not increase too much. If the fixed cost were to be independent of λ, then the profit-maximizing choice of quality is indicated by the point B in figure 2.8, where the quality choice is that which would be made by the margi-nal purchaser paying the marginal cost. In this case, the quality response of the supplier has the effect of increasing n_o, and hence of excluding a larger proportion of the population. It is of course possible that an increase in quality is profitable at all λ in the feasible range (in figure 2.8 this would mean that λ_{max} is to the left of B), and that the monopolist again produces λ_{max}, even though c/λ rises with λ.

To the extent, therefore, that economic progress leads to the invention of higher quality products, this may either reduce or increase the proportion of the population excluded from purchase of a good necessary to function.

Conclusion

The reader may well be saying that the results reported above depend on the strong assumptions made regarding the market structure. It is possible – although not guaranteed – that greater competition increases the range of goods available. This may be the case, but the main point of this account is to demonstrate the need to consider the conditions under which goods are supplied. The exclusion of consumers from the market depends on the working of the product market – of which we require a more sophisticated analysis.

2.5 Household Production, Time and the Take-Up Problem

In this final section, I turn to the inner workings of the household. The micro-economic theory of the household has developed a great deal, notably with the development of the theory of household production. A landmark of particular relevance here is the article by Gary Becker (1965) on the economics of the allocation of time. Central is the idea that goods are necessary not in themselves but to facilitate household activities (as in the previous section). Moreover, carrying out the activities requires time. These ideas have major implications for the definition of a poverty line conceived in terms of a minimum standard of living.

One of the two approaches to the definition of poverty adopted in the first Lecture took a basket of goods, x^*, and this was the base for the poverty line:

$$\pi = p \cdot x^* \tag{2.36}$$

This in turn has implications for the up-rating of the poverty line over time: it should be adjusted in line with the movement in prices (the weights in the price index being those of the poverty basket – it should not be a general price index for the whole population). The scale is fixed in real terms over time. Suppose now that we see goods, not as ends in themselves, but as a means to facilitating household activities. This perception of the household means that our ultimate concern is not with the quantities of goods consumed but with the level of activities achieved. The level of such activities I am going to denote by z, and it is this which is assumed to be the basis for our defined standard of living. The poverty standard involves a specified target, z^*. Such activities may be directly related to consumption, like having dinner, an activity which evidently requires a variety of goods inputs, both non-durable and durable, and requires time. Another example is 'going on holiday'. Or activities may be such things as 'going to work' or 'bringing up children'.

The idea of the household as a 'small factory', to use the phrase of Cairncross (1958), means that we have to consider the nature of the production function. Here for simplicity I am going to take the case of a linear technology,[14] where each activity requires a fixed vector of inputs, a_{ij} units of good i for each unit of the activity j. I assume that all consumption activities require the positive input of at least one good: there is no such thing as 'pure leisure'. If we denote the input–output matrix by A, the cost of achieving the target level of activities now becomes

$$\pi = p\, A\, z^* \tag{2.37}$$

and the level of the poverty line now depends on the technology A as well as prices, p. For future reference, I write the budget constraint of the household as

$$p\, A\, z^* \leq wL + b + m \tag{2.38}$$

where w denotes the hourly wage rate, L the hours of work (so wL is total earnings), b denotes benefit income, and m denotes other income (from savings). The formulation (2.37) has evident implications for the up-rating of the poverty line over time. Holding constant the level of activities, the poverty line may change in real terms on account of changes in the technology. One tends to think in terms of technical progress reducing costs, and this may happen, but there may well be factors working in the opposite direction, as I shall discuss in a moment. The central point is that the bundle of goods does not necessarily remain constant.

The household production approach provides a framework within which to clarify the distinction between absolute and relative poverty lines. A relative poverty line I interpret in this context to be one where the vector of activities is adjusted over time: for example, the introduction of a new activity of 'going on holiday', so that the vector z^* is extended. An absolute poverty line, on the other hand, is one where the vector of activities is constant; but the required spend-

14 One can look at this model as the polar opposite case from the linear characteristics model of Gorman (1956) and Lancaster (1966), where each unit of goods contributes to a range of different characteristics.

ing on goods may change in real terms because of changes in technology, A. The way in which the technology matrix may change in response to a rise in the general standard of living has been illustrated by Amartya Sen as follows:

> in West Europe or North America a child might not be able to follow his school programme unless the child happens to have access to a television. If this is in fact the case, then the child without a television in Britain or Ireland would be clearly worse off – have a lower standard of living – in this respect than a child, say, in Tanzania without a television. It is not so much that the British or the Irish child has a brand new need, but that to meet the same need as the Tanzanian child – the need to be educated – the British or the Irish child must have more commodities. (1984, pp. 336–7)

Introducing time

Goods are not the only inputs required to achieve a certain level of activity. Time is also important. Alongside the money budget constraint (2.38) is the time constraint

$$\tau.z \leq T - L \qquad (2.39)$$

where the elements of the vector τ denote the time required for each activity – eating dinner, going on holiday etc. All consumption activities are assumed to require a strictly positive input of time. T denotes the total available time, of which L is spent on work. At this point, I should note that I am talking about the household as if it consists of a single person.

The household is constrained by both income and time. If we assume that additional consumption of activities yields a positive benefit (the household is not satiated), then at most one of these constraints holds with an inequality. (If both held with a strict inequality, then one element at least of z could be increased, raising the consumption benefit of the household.) But can *one* of the constraints hold with inequality?

We have now the distinguish between the situation where the household can vary hours of work, L, freely and the situation where hours of work are constrained ($L = L_o$). If L can be freely varied, then the household can ease one constraint at the expense of the other, and we can in effect reduce them to a single constraint, holding with equality, in what Becker calls 'full income'. Suppose, for example, that the household had spare hours. Then more hours could be worked, generating earnings which would allow a higher level of consumption activities. Or, suppose that consumption were limited by available

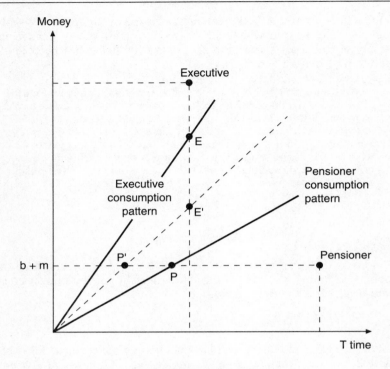

Figure 2.9 Time and money constraints.

time, but not money, then the household would choose to work less. Algebraically, where L is freely variable, we can multiply (2.39) by w and eliminate wL, to obtain the overall constraint

$$(p\ A + \tau w)\ z = wT + b + m \tag{2.40}$$

The left hand side measures the cost of activities, allowing both for goods and time costs (τw).

More relevant here is the case where the household is constrained to work a certain number of hours, which may be zero in the case of people who are unemployed. In that case we have to look in both dimensions, as in figure 2.9. The vertical axis measures the money available for spending on consumption activities, where this depends on the fixed number of hours, L_o; the horizontal measures the time which is available for these activities after working L_o hours. For each household, we may define a rectangle which delimits their possible consumption. Two illustrative examples are shown in figure 2.9.

The first is a pensioner not in paid work whose available time is equal to T and whose money income is $b + m$. The second is an executive, forced to work long hours, leaving little time for consumption despite a high money income. Suppose first that all households consume the same mix of activities regardless of prices or endowments. The overall level of benefit can then be measured by the distance along the dashed ray through the origin shown in figure 2.9.[15] The pensioner can attain the level P' and the executive the level E'. The pensioner is income-constrained and the executive cannot find the time to spend all income. Of course, in reality, the executive will try to substitute time-saving activities, buying in services, so that the actual consumption pattern is, say, that shown by the upper solid line, with consumption at point E. The pensioner will use spare time to seek activities which cost less in money, such as growing vegetables at home, allowing consumption at point P. But there are limits in both directions. Growing vegetables at home requires seeds and other goods inputs.

How is this related to the measurement of poverty? If the standard of living approach determines a specified set of activities, z^*, then people may be classified as 'money poor' or 'time poor' – see figure 2.10, where pAz^* corresponds to the goods requirements and $\tau.z^*$ corresponds to the time requirements. The people classified as money poor are those below the horizontal line. Of these people, some will sufficiently endowed with time, a group which may include pensioners and the unemployed. Others will also be short of time – those in the rectangle nearest the origin. And there will also be those who are above the poverty line in money terms but who do not have the time necessary to carry out the minimum level of activities. There may for example be people in jobs where the pay is only adequate if one works very long hours: for example, railway level crossing keepers in Britain working 60 or more hours a week. One conclusion that can be drawn is that we need to consider a category of people who are not money poor but *time poor*, as was argued by Clair Vickrey (1977).

How is this analysis helpful? Suppose that we return to the question of the effect of technical progress on the up-rating of the poverty line. In the 1960s theory of economic growth, there was a literature on the nature of technical progress. If there is no choice of

15 If the mix of activities is denoted by the vector $z^#$, then we can write

$$z = \theta \, z^#$$

where θ is the scale of operation. The slope of the dashed line in figure 2.9 is then

$$pAz^# / \tau \, z^#.$$

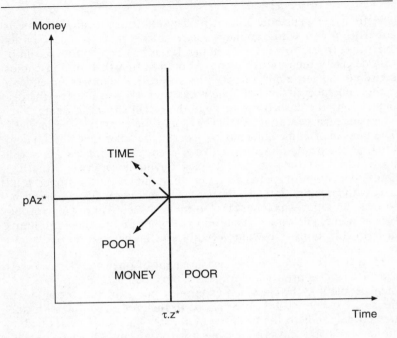

Figure 2.10 Time poor and money poor.

technique, as is the situation here with a single vector z^*, we have the question as to whether technical progress moves you inwards for both factors or whether it saves one factor but leads the technology to be more intensive in the other. Hicks, Harrod and others discussed this question in connection with aggregate economic growth (see, for example, Hahn and Matthews, 1964). In the present context, the question is illustrated in figure 2.10. Does technical progress move us in the direction of the solid arrow (lowering both necessary goods inputs and time inputs) or the dashed arrow (where time requirements are reduced but the required goods inputs are increased)? There are in fact some reasons to expect that innovations in household production technology have been time-saving but goods-using.[16] If technical changes have in fact taken us in this direction, then the real cost of the necessary basket of goods has increased, and this provides a further reason why the poverty line may have risen in real terms.

16 The role of time-saving technical change in the Industrial Revolution is discussed by von Tunzelmann (1995).

[104]

A second use of the model of household time allocation is to explore the problem of incomplete take-up of means-tested social assistance.

The take-up problem

For several countries in Europe there is evidence that people fall below the legal minimum income. In West Germany people fall below the level of *Sozialhilfe*; in the United Kingdom people are below the Income Support level; in Belgium people are below the Minimex level; in Ireland, people are below the Supplementary Welfare Allowance level. Leaving aside errors in the data, there are several reasons why this may happen:

(1)   The legal minimum may not cover all the population: for example, in the United Kingdom people working 16 or more hours a week do not (in 1997) qualify for Income Support;
(2)   There may be a liability to maintain by, for example, a son or daughter, which is not being fulfilled (or may not be captured in the statistics);[17]
(3)   People may not be claiming the assistance to which they are entitled.

Here I concentrate on the last of these.

There is evidence from a range of countries that incomplete take-up is a serious problem and that it is not readily overcome. In the United Kingdom, the shortcomings of the national safety net, then called National Assistance, were highlighted in *The Poor and the Poorest* by Abel-Smith and Townsend, who concluded that

> While it is impossible to give precise figures it is clear that substantial numbers in the population were not receiving national assistance in 1953–54 and 1960 and yet seemed, *prima facie*, to qualify for it. (1965, p. 64)

17 For example, in France and Germany there is a liability to maintain placed on ascendant and descendant relatives (Stevens, 1973, p. 51, Whittle, 1977, pp. 27–30 and 1978, pp. 17–18). In the United Kingdom, the issue of liability across generations has been highly controversial. The abolition of the household means test in the 1940s in legislation was described by de Schweinitz as 'one of the most dramatic and significant steps in the whole history of English relief' (1943, p. 223).

The government proceeded to initiate a specially designed survey of pensioners to establish the extent of non take-up in this group, and found that a sizeable proportion (39 per cent) of pensioners were not claiming the assistance to which they were entitled (Ministry of Pensions and National Insurance, 1966). As a consequence, a new scheme, Supplementary Benefit, was introduced to replace National Assistance. The changes in administration were intended to improve the take-up rate; however the analysis in Atkinson (1969) showed that more than half of the ensuing increase in the number of recipients could be attributed to the more generous scale rate rather than an improvement in take-up.

Incomplete take-up continues to be a problem in the United Kingdom. The official estimates for 1994/5, for example, show that between 76 per cent and 83 per cent of those apparently entitled were receiving Income Support.[18] Take-up was lowest among pensioners, for whom the estimated range was 59 per cent to 66 per cent, whereas that for lone parents was 95 per cent to 98 per cent Since the average entitlement of those not claiming is less than that of those claiming (Fry and Stark, 1987), the shortfall of expenditure is less: on an expenditure basis the overall take-up was between 88 per cent and 92 per cent (Department of Social Security, 1996a, Table 3.1). For pensioners, the take-up in terms of expenditure was 73 per cent to 79 per cent, the mean unclaimed amount being £14.10 a week.

Evidence about non take-up is more limited for other European countries. In the case of Denmark, Hansen and Hultin note that

> analysis of take-up rates has not been carried out regularly in Denmark. It is normally assumed that those who have a right to benefits also receive them. (1997, p. 15)

Yet they go on to estimate that, in the case of housing benefit, only 67 per cent of non-pensioners, and 85 per cent of pensioners, received the payments to which they were entitled in 1992. State expenditure would have been about 14 per cent higher if all benefit had been

---

18 It should be noted that there are a number of methodological problems in the measurement of take-up – see Atkinson (1989, ch. 11), Harris (1994) and Duclos (1995). The range given here allows a number of possible sources of error in the estimates – see Department of Social Security, 1996a, table 3.2, and, for earlier estimates, 1993a. Duclos (1997) has modelled the effect of benefit mis-reporting (i.e. not declaring receipt of assistance), of underestimation of entitlement by the benefit agency, and errors in the measurement of eligibility by the analyst. He concludes that the net effect is to raise the estimated take-up rate of Supplementary Benefit in 1985 from 64 per cent to 80 per cent.

claimed (1997, p. 47). In West Germany, statistics for the 1960s and 1970s suggested a take up rate for *Hilfe zum Lebensunterhalt* of around a half – see Hauser and Semrau (1990, p. 37). Their more recent estimates indicate that the take-up rate increased from 54 per cent in 1973 to 66 per cent in 1983, but the problem still remains serious. In the Netherlands, an analysis of administrative records for a means-tested supplement to the basic earnings-related benefit showed that 33 per cent of the unemployed did not claim and there is evidence of incomplete take-up for other benefits (van Oorschot, 1991). In Ireland, Callan et al. found that in 1987 the take-up of Supplementary Welfare Allowance was less than 50 per cent and they noted that it was

> not simply a matter of small amounts which potential claimants do not consider it worthwhile to claim. (1989, p. 148)

For other countries, there is material in the wide-ranging study of social assistance in twenty four countries carried out for OECD and the United Kingdom Department of Social Security by Eardley et al. (1996). They found that the take-up question

> is not one which has been extensively researched in Belgium, but there are indications that some of the problems exist which are familiar from research in other countries. (1996, Vol. II, p. 74)

For Austria, 'There are no reliable estimates available of the take-up rate for *Sozialhilfe*', but they quote one response to the expert questionnaire as saying

> that receipt of cash social assistance, as opposed to other social security benefits, is still highly stigmatising. (Eardley et al., 1996, Vol. II, p. 54)

In the case of Finland:

> The major obstacle to social assistance is linked to the image of the welfare agency; it is still a marginal service for 'marginal' people. . . . According to a national survey . . . , the majority of people felt it would be difficult to apply for social assistance because of the stigma attached to claiming. (Eardley et al., 1996, Vol. II, p. 141)

Problems of take-up also arise with programmes for those in work. A number of countries have introduced income-tested schemes for families with children. In the United Kingdom, when Family Income Supplement was first proposed, concern was expressed about the problem of incomplete take-up and the government set a target take-up rate of 85 per cent. The early numbers claiming did not suggest that this had been attained and examination of the time-series of numbers in receipt indicated no trend towards improved take-up (Atkinson and Champion, 1989). There was no evidence that advertising campaigns, such as that launched in 1976, had any appreciable impact on take-up. The official estimates for 1985–6 (Department of Social Security, 1989a, table 48.02) showed that in terms of numbers (a 'caseload basis') only 48 per cent of those eligible were claiming. In terms of expenditure, the take-up rate was 54 per cent (the unclaimed amount being on average 76 per cent of the average amount claimed).

One of the aims of Family Credit, which replaced FIS in 1988, was to increase take-up. Although the more recent estimates of take-up are higher, there is still considerable room for improvement. The official estimate of the take-up rate in 1994/5 on a caseload basis was 69 per cent (Department of Social Security, 1996a, table 4.2), and on an expenditure basis was 82 per cent (table 4.1). Nearly one family in three was apparently not claiming, and a fifth of the benefit was not claimed. The mean unclaimed amount was £23.40 a week. As was found by Marsh and McKay (1993), there is a lower take-up rate for couples than for single parents. In 1994/5 the take-up rate on a caseload basis was 80 per cent for single parents compared with 61 per cent for couples (Department of Social Security, 1996a, table 4.2). A Family Income Supplement scheme was introduced in Ireland in 1984 and estimates by Callan et al. indicate very low take-up rates:

> No more than about a quarter of eligible families appeared to be receiving the benefit, and no more than £3 to £4 out of every £10 of potential expenditure was claimed. (1995, p. 35)

The non take-up of benefits is often regarded with suspicion by economists. Why should people pass up what may be quite sizeable amounts of money or valuable benefits in kind? This behaviour scarcely accords with that assumed in other branches of public finance, such as the expected utility maximizing tax evader. But there are a number of explanations of the non take-up of transfers which are quite consistent with utility maximization. If, as the police chief said in the film *Casablanca*, we 'round up the usual suspects', then one of these is 'imperfect information'. It does indeed seem a probable explanation of incomplete take-up, since means-tested programmes are inherently complex. People may be unaware of the benefit, perhaps because they lack the skills of literacy or numeracy required to assimilate the information provided. They may be aware of its existence but not believe that they are entitled. This may happen where they have previously applied and have (correctly) been deemed ineligible but where there has been a subsequent change in the programme, or in their circumstances, which makes them eligible. Understanding the benefit system is not easy. The form required for Family Credit in the United Kingdom covers 16 pages, plus 4 pages for the employed or 6 pages for the self-employed, so that a couple with income from both sources face up to 26 pages plus an optional additional 4 pages for those with child-care costs! All of this requires an 10-page instruction book.

Lack of information has been the aspect seized on by the government, who have spent large sums on advertising. But evidence suggests that it is only part of the story. There is not, for example, any very clear upward trend over time in take-up as benefits become better known. A detailed analysis of the time-series for the means-tested programme for children in the United Kingdom showed no appreciable effect of advertising campaigns nor any significant upward time trend (Atkinson and Champion, 1989). Studies which have informed people of their entitlements have found that even when aware they do not claim.

This may appear irrational, but it is of course consistent with the household activity model with both money and time constraints. A benefit may raise a household above the money poverty line but at a cost in time which puts them into time poverty. In the case of the elderly, for example, the time cost may not be so large, but for those working long hours or single parents with the care of children the time cost may exceed the monetary benefit. Parents may be too busy to collect the necessary information and go through the claim process. Information has to be assembled on income and assets, as well as the other variables relevant to determining eligibility. This may not be easy. I can remember one family where the husband had just started as a fisherman, and he was asked to produce a certified statement of his expected profits over the next year! Just getting the forms signed – by one's partner, by the employer, by the child-minder or nursery manager – may be very time-consuming.

Time costs are not, however, the only explanation. Detailed studies of the motives for not claiming reveal that it is also related to the stigma associated with receipt of assistance. Potential recipients may be deterred by the way in which the benefit is administered and the treatment they receive from officials. They may not wish to reveal information to their employer: for example that they have a child. These kind of considerations take us outside those usually discussed by economists, and we may need to draw on psychology and other disciplines: see, for example, the review of recipient reactions to aid by Fisher et al. (1982). We need also to look at the behaviour of those administering the benefit and the role that they can play in facilitating or discouraging take-up. The explanation may lie as much on the supply as on the demand side.

The importance of the different reasons for non take-up is likely to vary across groups of the population and across countries. Matters such as stigma clearly depend on the particular culture and are influenced by historical experience. I return to these matters in Lecture 3 when considering the form of a European social minimum.

Concluding Comment

I began this Lecture by asking what economics can contribute to the study of poverty. I hope that the examples I have chosen show that economics does have helpful things to say and that I have indicated some of the ways in which there can be fruitful further research.

A central theme of the Lecture is the relation between poverty and social exclusion. Even if the aspects treated here are only some of the many dimensions of social exclusion, they serve as illustrations. A household below the legal minimum is excluded by a criterion of income poverty, and the proximate mechanism is the inadequate coverage of social insurance and the time cost of claiming the residual means-tested benefit (section 2.5). If, following the European Commission, we define exclusion with regard to the 'way of life', then investigation of the process must be extended to the conditions on which goods are supplied (section 2.3) and the availability of goods necessary to engage in activities carried out by the majority of people in society (section 2.4). Unemployment represents exclusion in a different sense (sections 2.1 and 2.2), where it may or may not coincide with financial poverty. The process of exclusion from the labour market is seen by some commentators as due to a social security system which induces people to reject labour market participation. By others it is seen as the outcome of exclusionary behaviour by trade unions or by employers setting a high profit hurdle for job creation.

Lecture 3

Political Economy of Poverty

The alleviation of poverty is seen by most modern governments as one of its a major responsibilities. This Lecture is concerned with the objectives and efficiency of anti-poverty policy. In part it is directed at the better design of such policies. Can we ensure that the poorest are protected against the rigours of macro-economic adjustment? Does the solution lie in better targeting of benefits? Can there be a concerted European effort to reduce poverty? But we have also to recognize that past policies have failed to eradicate poverty. Fifty years after Beveridge launched his attack on 'the giant evil of Want', people are still sleeping on the streets of Britain. We have therefore to be concerned with the analysis of poverty itself: the political economy of anti-poverty policy.

The first section (section 3.1) asks the question – What difference does it make to have an official poverty line? The existence of an official line (as in the United States) is often taken for granted, but how concretely does it affect policy? What is the impact of the European Commission 50 per cent of average poverty line? Why should the existence of an explicit target lead to a different outcome from the situation where the government simply acts as though there were a target? In order to explore this, I consider the theory of economic policy – both old-style and new-style – and its application to anti-poverty policy.

Viewed in a macro-economic light, there may appear to be an inevitable tension in Europe today between reducing poverty and achieving macro-economic stability, anti-poverty policy involving additional public spending, in flat opposition to the Maastricht criteria. Contemplation of this dilemma has led to enthusiasm for better targeting of social transfers. Redirection of transfers, it is claimed, allows them to be both cheaper and more effective. Targeting and efficiency in the alleviation of poverty are the subject of section 3.2. There are, however, a

[111]

number of problems with this approach. The scope for effective targeting is limited by administrative factors, by the impact on economic incentives, and by considerations of political economy, as is argued in section 3.3. If targeting does not offer a resolution of the dilemma, are there other paths which could be followed by welfare states in Europe? In order to explore this, we need to consider more fully the interrelation between social and economic policies, and the nature of the fiscal constraints. In section 3.4, I ask whether there is any scope for seeking to establish an effective European minimum which is consistent with Europe's other objectives, and, in section 3.5, I explore the form that such a minimum income might take, putting forward an alternative to the schemes typically considered.

3.1 The Political Economy of an Official Poverty Line

In the first Lecture, I made extensive reference to the European Commission's poverty criterion of 50 per cent of average income (or expenditure). This provides a highly salient point of reference in analysing the extent of poverty in Europe, but it also plays a role in the determination of policy. This role is relatively little discussed. What difference does it make to have an official standard? Does it have any significance that it has been designated officially in this way, rather than being simply the product of academic research?

In the United States, which has long had an official poverty line, the general opinion seems to be that it *does* make a difference. According to James Tobin, writing in 1970:

> The Federal 'war on poverty', whatever else it has accomplished, has established an official measure of the prevalence of poverty in the United States. Adoption of a specific quantitative measure, however arbitrary and debatable, will have durable and far-reaching political consequences. Administrations will be judged by their success or failure in reducing the officially measured prevalence of poverty. So long as any families are found below the official poverty line, no politician will be able to claim victory in the war on poverty or ignore the repeated solemn acknowledgements of society's obligations to its poorer members. (Tobin, 1970, p. 83)

This assessment was quoted approvingly some two decades later by Robert Haveman in his evaluation of the impact of social science research, where he says that:

> adoption of the 'Orshansky line' as the official measure of poverty represents an important example of the effect of research, combined with a certain amount of political compromise, on policy-making. (1987, p. 55)

[112]

In Ireland, in 1997, the Government adopted a National Anti-Poverty Strategy, as a follow up to the United Nations Social Summit in Copenhagen in 1995. This went further than agreeing on a poverty standard: it set a target for poverty reduction:

> Over the period, 1997–2007, the National Anti-Poverty Strategy will aim at considerably reducing the numbers of those who are 'consistently poor' from 9 per cent to 15 per cent to less than 5 to 10 per cent, as measured by the ESRI. (National Anti-Poverty Strategy, 1997, p. 9)

(The ESRI measures of poverty are those discussed in Lecture 1.) What is the role of such targets and how exactly do they make a difference? I examine these questions from a theoretical point of view, starting from an 'old-style' view of the theory of economic policy.

The theory of economic policy

The classic theory of economic policy is that associated with Tinbergen (1952 and 1954). Although this theory may today be regarded as rather old-fashioned when compared with the modern game-theoretic treatment of policy-making, I believe that it can make a valuable contribution to clarifying our thinking.

The first question concerns the distinction, drawn by Tinbergen, between *fixed* and *flexible* targets. The former specifies policy objectives in absolute terms. Policy must ensure that the balance of payments is in equilibrium or that the borrowing requirement does not exceed x per cent of national income. These are fixed targets. In contrast, a flexible target is one that indicates the direction in which we are aiming but where it is recognized that there may be limits to the extent that it can be attained. We may then have to trade gains in one direction against losses in another.

The stance adopted by western governments towards the alleviation of poverty seems to be better described as a flexible rather than a fixed target. Governments recognize a social obligation, but its attainment is limited on account of the constraints faced and the trade-off with other objectives. Beveridge may have claimed in his 1942 Plan that the level of the subsistence standard determined the level of social insurance benefits, but in reality the choice of target was influenced by what was feasible. Behind his proposals lay a balancing of the benefit levels with considerations of cost and incentive constraints. Beveridge claimed that the level of the subsistence standard determined the level of social insurance benefits, but in reality the choice of target was influenced by what was feasible.

[113]

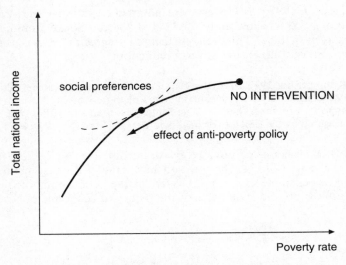

Figure 3.1 Policy trade-off between poverty
rate and total national income.

It does not in fact seem reasonable to see the elimination of poverty as a fixed target. Rather, it is a flexible target, the attainment of which is limited on account of the constraints faced by the government. These constraints in turn are unlikely to be absolute, but rather to involve a trade-off between different objectives. The government may in this case set the transfer payments at a level below the poverty line, because to raise them further would reduce other indicators of performance to a level it considers unsatisfactory. As it was put by the British government,

> Even if it were possible to arrive at some general consensus on a minimum acceptable income, this would not necessarily provide a determination of the level of benefits to be paid. . . . rates are not set in isolation: the Government gives due regard to the relationship between benefit levels and the rewards available to those in work, and to the total resources available for public spending. (Department of Social Security, 1989, p. 5)

To make the discussion more concrete, let us suppose that anti-poverty policy reduces poverty, but at the cost of higher taxes which have an adverse effect on total national income. There is an efficiency/equity trade-off as shown in figure 3.1: the larger the scale of expenditure on the anti-poverty programme, the more we move round the frontier (solid line) in an anti-clockwise direction. We then have to consider how much aggregate income we are willing to sacrifice in order to reduce poverty from, say, 15 to 10 per cent? The answer is given, on the Tinbergen approach, by a social welfare function defined over the level of the national income and the level of poverty. A person unconcerned about poverty would choose the 'no intervention' point in figure 3.1, with maximum national income. A person who was concerned about poverty would choose a point such as that shown by the tangency of the social preference contour (dashed curve) with the feasibility frontier.

This framework is quite illuminating. The United Kingdom, for example, in the 1980s witnessed a rise in total income and a rise in poverty. In terms of figure 3.1, there was a move upwards and to the right. If all that had happened had been a neutral improvement in the possibility set, then we should have expected an improvement on both fronts (assuming that both objectives are normal goods), so that the move would have been upwards and to the left. With this formulation of objectives and constraints, the observed policy development can only be explained if there had been either a shift in social preferences against poverty reduction (a change in the shape of the indifference curves) or a change in the shape of the feasibility frontier, with poverty reduction becoming more expensive.

The observed development of policy in the United Kingdom may reflect objectives different from those posited: for example, people may judge the degree of redistribution relative to the inequality of gross incomes. As much 'effort' is being put into poverty alleviation; it is just that the problem is larger. Indeed one conclusion may be that mainstream welfare economics is not adequate for our purposes. Concern with poverty does not follow, at least directly, from the standard formulation of policy objectives. Viewed from the standpoint of welfare economics, maximization of a Bergson–Samuelson social welfare function does not of itself imply that weight is attached to ensuring that people are above a poverty line. It is not a feature of a utilitarian objective, nor of more general functions taking individual welfares as their arguments, that special significance is attached to any particular level of income or welfare. The weighting of marginal increases in income implied by the social welfare function may, of course, mean that priority is given to transfers to those at the bottom of the income scale, as in the 'general redistributive preference' in figure 1.10. The extreme case of priority is that of the Rawlsian difference principle under which the welfare of the least advantaged is maximised. But this is not the same as concern with a poverty standard. This may be seen from the fact that it is conceivable that poverty is zero (for example, no one has an income below half the mean), so that total income is the sole

[115]

concern, whereas on a Rawlsian criterion it is the lowest income that remains the objective.

In order to give a role to poverty, we have to introduce the specific concern for those below the poverty line which was discussed in section 1.4.

Poverty line and the new theory of economic policy

So far I have sought to relate the official poverty objective to the old-fashioned theory of economic policy. More recently, the theory has taken a different course. As described by Torsten Persson and Guido Tabellini in their survey of *Macroeconomic Policy, Credibility and Politics*:

> In contrast to most earlier work, the new work treats the government as responding to incentives, not to orders. ... It specifies a government objective and views equilibrium policy as the optimal choice given the objective and various constraints. This approach leads to positive models of economic policy in alternative institutional environments. (1990, p. ix)

Such an approach resembles that adopted, in a public finance context, by public choice theorists, associated particularly with James Buchanan and Gordon Tullock. It leads us to ask what role would be played in the positive analysis of policy formation by an official poverty target? Why should any government accept such a target and what would be its implications? Would the existence of an official poverty line make any difference?

Economists often pride themselves on not being interested in rhetoric. It is not relevant what people *say* they do; all that matters is what they actually *do*. We can infer from their actions what are their preferences, and listening to what they state to be their objectives makes no difference to our understanding. On the other hand, many non-economists believe that stated objectives are relevant, and that it may be useful to distinguish between these and the preferences which appear to underlie the observed policy choices. Why should this be? Why should the existence of an explicit target lead to a different outcome from the situation where the government simply acts as though there were a target?

The answer clearly depends on the model of behaviour supposed to apply to the government. Many such models have been proposed and there is little consensus as to the most appropriate. Moreover, the most appropriate model is likely to vary over space and time. Here I take a starkly simplified approach. Suppose that there are two political parties concerned with being in power, and with

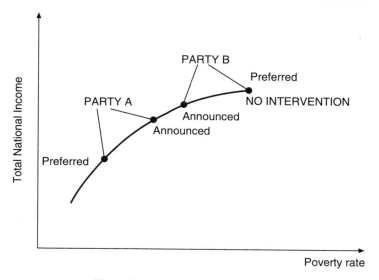

Figure 3.2 Choice of party platform.

achieving their interests, which are different for the two parties. (The model is based on that of two party competition described by Alesina (1988).) In order to dramatize the situation, suppose that one party, A, has a strong preference for an extensive anti-poverty programme, as shown in figure 3.2 and that the other, B, is only concerned with total income. Suppose, furthermore, that policy can be represented along the single dimension of the level of anti-poverty policy, which is a big 'if' and the Achilles' heel of this approach (once there is more than one dimension the existence of a majority voting equilibrium becomes highly problematic). Voters have preferences over different levels of transfers and the implied tax rate. As far as the parties are concerned, the outcome of the election is uncertain, and each acts as though the probability of winning is a function of the chosen policies of the two parties. The form of the function is assumed to be such that a party can increase its chance of election by converging towards the policy of its opponent.[1]

In such a situation, one would expect to find a convergence of

1 Denoting the policy of party A by X_A, and that of party B by X_B, in the region where $X_A > X_B$, the probability of election of party A is a declining function of X_A and the probability of election of party B is an increasing function of X_B.

political programmes, but not complete convergence.[2] Neither political party will pursue the policy which maximizes its own objective function, since it recognizes that some compromise will increase the probability of winning the election. On the other hand, the convergence is less than complete because parties attach some weight to their own objectives. Party B will propose a benefit level less than that of party A even though closing the gap would raise its probability of winning, since it would reduce the value of winning (being committed to a higher benefit level than it believes desirable).

What role would a poverty target play in these circumstances? Why should either party espouse such a target? It may appear obvious why the party A would establish such a target, since it is concerned about poverty, but why should the party B accept an official poverty objective, when it is opposed to anti-poverty policy? One answer lies in the kind of argument which macro-economists have been making in recent years: that there may be problems with the time consistency of policy. The description of the electoral competition assumed that political parties are pre-committed to a policy, whereas once elected they may in fact decide to follow their own preferences and not the policy on which they campaigned. If party B wins, it could then set transfers to zero, even if it had promised to maintain a certain level. As argued by Alesina (1988), if voters are rational, they take this into account, and in the limit they disregard the announced platforms. The outcome simply depends on the preferred choices of the political parties.

In such a situation, however, it may be in the interest of political parties to try and persuade voters that they will not act purely in their own interests once elected. In particular, party B may want to pre-commit itself to spend more than zero. The adoption of an official poverty line may represent a pre-commitment of this type. By announcing this target, party B may bind itself not to cut benefits, and the sophisticated electorate will therefore find it more acceptable, since it will remain closer to its campaign promises. This provides one argument why a party on the right would find it in its own

---

2 Denoting by $p(X_A, X_B)$ the probability of election of party A, and by $U_A(X)$ the utility of party A if policy X is followed, then if the party maximizes

$$p\ U_A(X_A) + (1-p)\ U_A(X_B)$$

then the derivative with respect to X_A is

$$p\ U'_A(x_A) - [U_A(X_A) - U_A(X_B)]\{-\partial p/\partial X_A\}$$

It follows that the policy chosen lies between X_B and that which maximizes $U_A(X)$.

interests to adopt a poverty target. Paradoxically, it is the party not concerned about poverty which adopts the poverty target. (Equally, it can explain the adoption of no-tax-increase pledges by parties on the left.)

What about party A? Party A finds it in its own interest to pre-commit itself not to spend as much on benefits as it would like, and here the announcement of a poverty target may worsen rather than improve its prospects. Such a pre-commitment would simply confirm voters in their suspicions that party A would be profligate with their money. On the other hand, the policy choice of the opposition is closer to its own preference. The adoption of a commitment may in fact make both parties better off.

In the model of party platform choice, there is no guarantee that the electoral equilibrium without pre-commitment is Pareto-efficient. There may well be a range of policies, lying between the extreme 'party preferred' choices, which are considered better by all members of the electorate. The existence of the pre-commitment means that they are offered a different set of policies, and a choice between the 'announced' policies in figure 3.2 may be seen as better than a choice between the more extreme policies. Voters may be better off – although there is no presumption that this is the case. It is also possible that voters, as well as politicians, can benefit from being tied like Ulysses to the mast. One's higher self may exhibit concern for the poor, whereas one's lower self may consult only private interest. In one's higher thinking, one may be persuaded by arguments based on concern for others, but when it comes to an election one may only take account of self interest. Recognizing our weakness, we may in this situation prefer, according to our higher selves, to be pre-committed to a policy which takes account of poverty. Put another way, the existence of an official poverty line may limit the range of policies which are put to the electorate. Voters are not exposed to temptation.

I have explored some of the ways in which political economy considerations affect the framing of government objectives; I turn now to the ways in which these objectives are pursued.

3.2 Targeting of Social Transfers and Efficiency in Alleviating Poverty

If the European Union is to achieve a reduction in poverty, while also attaining its Maastricht budgetary criteria, then many commentators have concluded that this requires greater targeting of government spending on social transfers, which constitute a major part of the budget in all EU countries. One such example is the paper on

'Growth and Employment: The Scope for a European Initiative', prepared by Jacques Drèze and Edmond Malinvaud (1994), on the basis of discussions with a group of Belgian and French economists. While emphasizing the positive functions of the welfare state, Drèze and Malinvaud contend that total spending should be cut by focusing benefits on those in need. Targeting is a politically attractive idea. However, calls for greater targeting need to be treated with caution. The argument in favour has to be made explicit and critically examined. Behind such policy recommendations lie views with regard to (a) the objectives of policy, (b) the range of instruments available to attain those objectives, and (c) the constraints under which policy has to operate (economic, political and social).

The first reason for caution is that the social security system has other important functions besides poverty alleviation. These include:

1 The smoothing of income over the life-cycle in relation to people's needs;
2 Provision of insurance against adversities, such as sickness, disability, unemployment or bereavement (where these involve a loss of income but not necessarily poverty); and
3 Redistribution towards those with dependents such as children, or disabled or elderly relatives.

These Lectures are about poverty, so that these other objectives are not discussed here, but evidently they must be taken into account in any assessment of the overall 'efficiency' of the social security system. Expenditure which is considered poorly 'targeted' when judged solely by the objective of alleviating poverty may well be directed at other objectives of the social security system. This might hardly seem worth saying, but much of recent debate seems to have lost sight of the fact that the relief of poverty is only one of the objectives of the transfer system. Indeed, historically in a number of western countries it was not even the most important motive for the introduction of transfers: for example, in France:

> social security was never primarily conceived as a tool to fight poverty. Security, in terms of protection against the risks and hazards of life, was its first, paramount objective. (Jallade, 1988, p. 248)

The objective was seen less in individualistic terms and more in terms of solidarity. In what follows, the reader should bear in mind that social security has wider objectives than the alleviation of poverty on which I focus here.

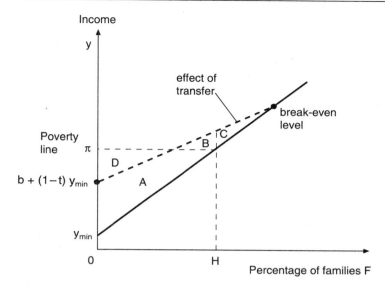

Figure 3.3   Measuring target efficiency.

Efficiency in alleviating income poverty

Suppose now that we consider only the objective of alleviating income poverty, or raising people to a specified poverty line, π, expressed in terms of income per equivalent adult using an appropriate equivalence scale. The approach commonly taken to the measurement of efficiency may be illustrated by reference to figure 3.3, where all families are ranked in increasing order of income along the horizontal axis. The solid line shows the income corresponding to a given percentile point in the distribution, so that for each proportion of the population, F, we can read off the highest income, y, found among the bottom F per cent. The lowest observed income is denoted by y_{min}. (The diagram is the inverse of the more usual cumulative distribution.) The diagram is drawn for the special case where the density function is uniform for y greater than or equal to y_{min}, so that the cumulative distribution, shown by the solid line, is a linear function of y. The distance between the solid line and the dotted line where $y = \pi$ measures the extent of shortfall from the poverty line, or the individual family's poverty gap. The aggregate poverty deficit is measured by the total area between these lines.

Figure 3.3 is based on the diagram given by Beckerman (1979, 1979a), who defines the 'poverty reduction efficiency' of transfers as the extent to which they reduce the poverty gap. Suppose that the solid line in figure 3.3 represents the situation before transfers and the dashed line the cumulative distribution after transfers. Everyone is better off up to the break-even level of income (no account is taken here of the financing of the transfers.) The reduction in the poverty gap is then indicated by the area A, and the poverty reduction efficiency of the transfers is measured by Beckerman by the ratio of the area A to the total transfer (A + B + C). The efficiency is less than 100 per cent to the extent that there are payments to the non-poor (C) and that there are 'excess' payments to the poor (B). The estimates of Beckerman for four countries in the 1970s show the following results for the efficiency of total social security spending: Australia 56 per cent, Great Britain 49 per cent, Norway 44 per cent and Belgium 8 per cent (1979a, table 19).

Belgium appears on this basis to do less well than the other three countries. This is, however, only part of the story. A programme could score well on poverty reduction efficiency but still leave a high level of poverty. The dashed line in figure 3.3 could be shifted vertically downwards until the break-even point coincided with the poverty line, eliminating the areas B and C. Nevertheless the poverty gap would still remain substantial. Alternatively, a relief programme could fill the poverty gap, but only for a fraction of those below the poverty line. It was this consideration which led Weisbrod (1970) to introduce the distinction between *vertical* and *horizontal* efficiency:

> Two issues are involved, having to do with the accuracy of the program in assisting *only* the 'target' group, and the comprehensiveness of the program in assisting *all* of that group. (1970, p. 125)

The former – vertical efficiency – is that already discussed. The latter – horizontal efficiency – is defined by Weisbrod as

> the ratio of benefits going to the target group to the total benefits 'needed' by that group. (1970, p. 125)

In terms of figure 3.3, horizontal efficiency is measured by the ratio of the area A to (A + D). For the four countries studied by Beckerman (1979a, table 19), the horizontal efficiency of the social security programme was 74 per cent in Australia, 92 per cent in Norway, 96 per cent in Great Britain, and 99 per cent in Belgium. This gives a rather different picture, in part because of differences in the total level of spending.

The vertical and horizontal efficiency indicators above have been based on the poverty gap. Alternatively, they could be defined on the basis of the headcount measure of poverty. As Weisbrod noted, the indicator of horizontal efficiency is then

> the ratio of the number of beneficiaries in the target group to the total number of persons in the target group. (1970, p. 125)

This indicator will lead to different answers. The programme represented by the dashed line in figure 3.3 achieves 100 per cent horizontal efficiency measured in this way, since all those below the poverty line benefit, and the same would be true if the dashed line were to be shifted vertically downwards until the break-even point coincided with the poverty line. Notions of 'efficiency' are not independent of the way in which we choose to measure poverty.

Explicit formulation of the poverty alleviation problem

Vertical and horizontal efficiency are therefore valuable indicators, but they are not on their own sufficient to guide policy formation. After all, a high level of horizontal efficiency may be achieved at great total cost; and we have seen that the value taken by the indicators depends on the choice of poverty measure. The indicators need to be related to the overall policy problem, with an explicit formulation of the objective and constraints. The statement that a particular programme has x per cent efficiency can only be interpreted in the context of such an explicit formulation.

Suppose that the government aims to maximize the poverty reduction achieved with a given budget,[3] and that, initially, the degree of poverty is measured by the normalized poverty gap, which is given algebraically by

$$G = (1/n) \, \Sigma_i \, [(\pi - y_i)/\pi] \tag{3.1}$$

where the sum is taken over those people with incomes below π, n denotes the total number of people, and the poverty gap has been normalized by dividing by the poverty line. The policy aim is to minimize G subject to a government budget constraint. In general, this constraint has to take account of changes in behaviour by the recipients of transfers. Recipients may spend part of the transfer on taxed goods, generating additional indirect tax revenue, or on those subsidised by the government, increasing public spending. The beneficiaries may adjust their labour supply behaviour, affecting the re-

---

3 This problem has been studied by, among others, Kanbur (1987), Ravallion and Chao (1989), and Bourguignon and Fields (1990).

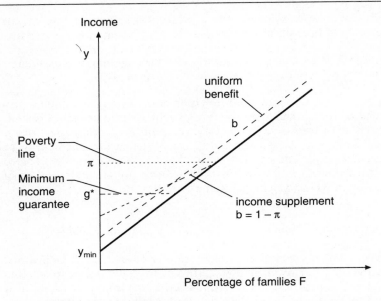

Figure 3.4 Three special cases of transfer programmes.

ceipts from income and other taxation. For the present, these second-round effects are not taken into account, it being assumed that the cost of a transfer is measured simply by the difference between pre-transfer and post-transfer incomes. (Possible changes in labour supply are considered in section 3.3.)

In this context, let us consider the class of transfer programmes represented by the dashed line in figure 3.3. If y denotes pre-transfer income, then net income is equal to a guaranteed income, b, minus a tax rate, t, times the pre-transfer income, with a break-even level at b/t. The intercept on the vertical axis shows the net income received by a family with the lowest pre-transfer income (equal to y_{min}). Three special cases are shown in figure 3.4. The first case is that of a uniform benefit ($t = 0$), shown by the dashed line. Where t is positive, then the benefit may be said to be 'income-targeted'. The second special case is where the break-even level is set at the poverty line, so that $b = t\,\pi$. This case, referred to as an 'income supplement', eliminates the poverty reduction inefficiency associated with the areas B and C in figure 3.3, since transfers are limited to those below the poverty line, and the transfer is less than the individual poverty gap. The same is true of the third special case where $t = 1$, which provides a 'minimum income guarantee', g^*, which concentrates the transfer on the poorest, with net income becoming g^* for all y less than or equal to g^*.

[124]

How do these transfer programmes fare when compared according to the explicit poverty alleviation problem? To illustrate the comparison, let us take a simple numerical example which, while artificial, provides a useful laboratory within which to explore the quantitative magnitudes. The example takes a poverty line of half average family income. It assumes a uniform distribution of incomes over the relevant range upwards from zero income (i.e. $y_{min} = 0$). Taking the headcount as 30 per cent. the poverty gap is then 7½ per cent of total income.[4] The impact of the different schemes obviously depends on whether the total budget is sufficient to eliminate all poverty. If the budget allowed the poverty gap to be completely filled by a guaranteed income equal to π, then this policy could not be bettered. In what follows, it is assumed that the available budget is less than the total poverty gap. Suppose in fact that the total budget is 2½ per cent of total income, allowing an income supplement of 33⅓ per cent, a uniform payment equal to 5 per cent of the poverty line, and a minimum income guarantee of 57.7 per cent of the poverty line,[5] or 28.85 per cent of average income.

Where the poverty measure takes the form of the poverty gap, the income supplement, or any other transfer limited to those below the poverty line, achieves the maximum reduction in poverty subject to the budget constraint. The value of the objective function is reduced to $(1-t)$ of its previous value, or by 33⅓ per cent with our numerical example. The reduction achieved by the uniform transfer is considerably less: the gap falls by a factor $(1 - b^*/(\pi-y_{min}))^2$, which from the budget constraint is equal to $(1 - Ht/2)^2$. In the numerical example, the value of the objective function is reduced only by some 10 per cent. Where the problem of poverty is that of a minority, the universal transfer does not score well on this measure of efficiency.

If, instead of the poverty gap, we consider the class of poverty measures proposed by Foster et al. (1984), used in Lecture 1, with a parameter, a:[6]

---

4 With a uniform distribution, and a lowest income equal to zero, the poverty gap is $H\pi/2$, where H is the head-count.

5 The cost of the minimum income guarantee is $(H/\pi)(g^*)^2/2$, which is equal to $(g^*/\pi)^2$ times the poverty gap. With a budget equal to one third of the poverty gap, the guarantee which can be financed is $\sqrt{(1/3)}$ of the poverty line.

6 This expression differs from that proposed by Foster et al. (1984), and from that generally used, in that P is expressed to the power of a. This is to ensure that, as a tends to infinity, the measure converges to the Rawlsian form. It may be noted that, with a uniform continuous density h, integrating to unity over the whole range, the expression P is equal to

$$[h\pi/(1 + a)]^{1/a} [1-y_{min}/\pi]^{1+1/a}$$

so that it converges to $[1-y_{min}/\pi]$ as a tends to infinity.

$$(P_a)^a = (1/n) \sum_i [(\pi - y_i)/\pi]^a \qquad \text{where } a \geq 1 \tag{3.2}$$

then the reduction in the objective function continues to be a factor of $(1-t)$ with the income supplement, but that from the uniform transfer is $(1 - b^*/(\pi - y_{min}))^{1+1/a}$, which falls with a. Where a equals 2, the reduction in poverty achieved by the uniform transfer falls to 7½ per cent. In the limit, as a approaches infinity, all weight is attached to the poverty gap of the poorest person, which is reduced by 5 per cent with the uniform payment.

It is also clear that, where the government attaches more weight to larger poverty gaps, the minimum income guarantee is more effective than the income supplement as a means of poverty reduction. Where a equals 2, the reduction in poverty achieved by the minimum income guarantee rises to 38 per cent. On this basis, the minimum income guarantee is 15 per cent better than the income supplement. As a rises towards infinity, approaching a Rawlsian concern with only the least advantaged, the level of poverty reduction with the minimum income guarantee reaches 57.7 per cent, compared with 33⅓ per cent with the income supplement. If the lowest pre-transfer income is zero, then the policies are ranked according to their intercept with the vertical axis in figure 3.4.

The 'sharpness' of objectives

The crucial role played by the form of social objectives in this field may lead us to be more questioning about their formulation. The efficiency advantage of the income supplement arises because we are agreed that the poverty line is π. A marginal Euro received by a person above π is valued at zero. Such a 'sharp' representation of social objectives may not, however, be universally accepted. There may well be disagreement about the location of the poverty line, as discussed in the first Lecture. What one person may see as 'wasteful' expenditure on the non-poor, another may regard as contributing to the reduction of poverty. Alternatively, there may be agreement about the location of π, but concern for the 'near-poor', or the group above but close to the poverty line.

A wider distributional objective – while still concerned with poverty – may give some weight to transfers received within a range of the poverty line. Following the procedure of Ribich (1968), we may set a higher level so that transfers within a certain distance of the poverty line receive a positive weight (although less than that below the poverty line). Another approach, that explored here, is to combine a 'high' value of the poverty line with a form of the objective function (3.2) and values of the parameter a greater than 1, shading

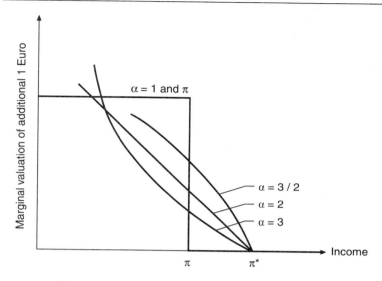

Figure 3.5   A less 'sharp' poverty objective.

the poverty objective, allowing differential weights to be attached to different poverty gaps. The implied marginal valuation of income for different people is illustrated in figure 3.5. The sharp heavy line of the poverty gap below π is replaced by one of the lines marked by different values of a starting from the higher poverty line π^*.

With such a less sharp objective, the relative efficiency of the different transfer schemes is changed. We have seen that with the adoption of a value of the parameter · greater than 1, the minimum income guarantee (and the income supplement) become more efficient. The raising of the poverty line, on the other hand, has the opposite impact. A rise in the poverty line brings with it a rise in the number of beneficiaries from the uniform transfer who are 'deserving' according to the poverty criterion, but no increase in the effectiveness of the minimum income guarantee, which remains fixed at g^* (the total budget being held constant). In relative terms, the poverty reduction falls for both transfer programmes, but the fall is much larger for the minimum income guarantee. Suppose for example that we take a equal to 2, a value commonly used in empirical work. The minimum income remains at the same level as before in our example, which is 28.85 per cent of average income; the uniform transfer is 2.5 per cent of average income. With the poverty line set at 50 per cent of average income, the efficiency of the minimum income guarantee is such that it reduces the poverty measure by 38 per cent, compared with 7.5 per cent for the uniform transfer, an advantage of some 5 to 1. On the other hand, if we take a 'high' poverty line of 75 per cent of average income, then the reduction achieved by the minimum income guarantee becomes 18 per cent, compared with 5 per cent with the uniform transfer. The relative superiority of the minimum income guarantee is still sizeable but is reduced to 3½ to 1 when we adopt this less sharp objective.

Lack of sharpness in objectives affects not simply the aggregate poverty measure, but also applies to the assessment of individual welfare. There is, for example, potential disagreement about the treatment of earned incomes. As emphasized by Kanbur, Keen and Tuomala (1990), and Besley and Coate (1992), there is a difference between evaluating the position of individuals in terms of their *consumption* and evaluating their *utility*, where the latter takes account of the disutility of work. To make the point, we may note that corresponding to a constant elasticity labour supply function with elasticity β, and no income effect (used later in section 3.4):

$$\ell = w^\beta \tag{3.3}$$

where w is the wage rate, the level of indirect utility can be written as

$$v = w\,\ell/(1+\beta) + m \tag{3.4}$$

where m denotes benefit and other (unearned) income. It is the level of indirect utility that would enter a 'welfarist' measure of poverty, with labour income being discounted by a factor $(1 + \beta)$, which allows for the cost of working. In contrast, as Kanbur, Keen and Tuomala point out, the policy debate tends to give no weight to the disutility of effort, and the individual situation is evaluated in terms of $w\ell + m$. The difference between these two valuations can affect the conclusions drawn regarding working families: the group identified as below a specified poverty line is different.

A second, related, example is that, as discussed in section 2.5, the claiming of benefits may involve costs for the recipient, either of time or money. There is then a question as to whether these costs should be deducted. Individuals may evaluate their welfare, and base their decision whether or not to claim, on the net position, but the government may determine their poverty status according to their gross income, if only because the cost may be difficult to measure. Again, the 'policy' definition excludes some people who consider their own welfare level to be below that attainable with a cash benefit of π.

Behind these examples lies the more general question of the dimension of poverty with which we are concerned. A move from income poverty to measures based on other dimensions may lead to signifi-

Table 3.1 Errors in targeting in using income in place of expenditure

	'correct'	Type I error (false negatives)	Type II error (false positives)
Germany	8.5	3.5	5.1
United Kingdom	12.4	4.5	10.0
Netherlands	1.7	4.5	5.7
Denmark	2.4	1.9	9.5
Ireland	8.0	8.4	6.9
Spain	6.8	10.7	6.1

Source: Hagenaars et al. (1994), table A4.5.

cant changes in the recommendations regarding anti-poverty policy. Use of consumption rather than income as a criterion for identifying those in poverty will lead to a population which overlaps only in part with those defined as poor on an income basis. Suppose that our object is to help households in Europe with expenditures below 50 per cent of the mean, but that we have to target using income as the criterion (i.e. those with incomes below 50% of the mean income qualify). From the estimates of Hagenaars et al. (1994) we can calculate, as shown in table 3.1, the proportions of Type I errors, or 'false negatives', where eligible families are not awarded benefit, and Type II errors, or 'false positives', where benefits are awarded to those not eligible. Both the latter figures are quite large relative to the number for whom income is a correct indicator of expenditure status. These estimates cannot of course tell us how any actual transfer scheme would operate, but they are a warning that the case for targeting on a single poverty index, measured in terms of income, becomes weaker if we allow for differences in view as to the object of redistribution.

Conclusion

The aim of this section has been to set out the theoretical argument which is implicit in many of the calls for greater targeting, and to show how the assessment of relative efficiency depends on the formulation of social objectives and the constraints under which they can be achieved. The statement that a particular programme has x per cent efficiency can only be interpreted in the context of such an explicit formulation of objectives and constraints. The attractiveness of targeting depends on how narrowly defined are the objectives of policy, and on how much agreement there is about the form of those objectives. A highly targeted income guarantee may perform less well when judged according to less sharp criteria and according to objectives other than the alleviation of income poverty.

3.3 The Limits of Targeting via Means Tests

When people talk of targeting, they usually have in mind the replacement of universal schemes by benefits which are subject to tests of income and assets. Means-tested assistance replaces social insurance or categorical benefits (like child benefit). In this section, I identify some of the problems with the use of targeting in this form. The scope for governments to target benefits effectively is limited not just by the budgetary cost, which has been the sole constraint taken into account in the previous section, but also by administrative factors, by the impact on economic incentives, and by considerations of political economy.

Imperfect information

Imperfect targeting may arise on account of errors in administration. The conditions for receipt of a transfer such as child benefit may be perfectly aligned with social objectives, but the existence of the programme may not be known to all those potentially eligible, or people may make false claims which are not detected. Imperfect targeting may also arise because the conditions of benefit are only imperfectly correlated with the objectives. Restriction of an income-related family benefit to those not in full-time work will mean that the families of low-paid workers may still be in poverty.

Where the correlation is less than perfect, or where there are errors in the identification of the categories, then this may lead to the false negatives referred to above, where eligible families are not awarded benefit, and to false positives, where benefits are awarded to those not eligible (Goodin, 1985). The awarding of benefits to those not eligible reduces the vertical efficiency of the programme; the exclusion of eligible families leads to horizontal inefficiency in that the programme becomes less effective in covering the poor. Seen in terms of poverty minimization, false positives add to the cost with no benefit (just as with the universal transfers paid to the non-poverty population), and false negatives reduce both costs and benefits.

This brings me to the role of information. In the operation of a transfer programme, there is often an asymmetry of information in that the needs of the individual are known to him or her but not to the administering agency. There may also be third parties, like employers, who have the necessary information. There is then a 'principal-agent' problem in the design of transfers, where the aim of the government is to induce all of those eligible to claim and to ensure that all of those who claim are in fact eligible.

It is possible to imagine circumstances in which there is no problem of information. *If* the government operates a personal income tax, *if* everyone files a tax return, and *if* this information is deemed sufficient to determine the payment, then in theory it would be possible for the agency to identify from the income tax records those people with low incomes, calculate the necessary benefit amount, and *if* the administrative machinery exists, to mail a payment to the beneficiary. In the United States, the earned income tax credit for families with dependents operates by making payments to those whose income tax returns reveal that their earned income is below a certain level (and satisfy a condition on total income). In this situation, one

[131]

could operate an 'automatic' income-related programme. However, these conditions are highly unlikely to be satisfied. The obligation to file a tax return may not be enforced among those who are likely to have incomes below the tax threshold. In the case of the United States earned income credit, this means that a number of those potentially eligible do not benefit (Seidman, 1990, p. 92; and Scholz, 1994). The typical transfer programme depends on categorical criteria as well as income-eligibility. Information necessary to verify these categorical conditions may not be contained on the income tax return: for example, that in the United Kingdom does not (in 1997) include details of the number of children. Information on income in the past tax year, the basis for paying the US earned income credit, will not allow urgent current needs to be met. The US scheme does include provisions for the credit to be claimed in advance, but this has to be initiated by the recipient.

It seems likely, therefore, that any actual income-related transfer programme will not be automatic. Payment will require action on the part of the claimant. There are then two important stages: the decision by the potential beneficiary to make a claim, and the verification by the government of the claim. The first of these may be considered purely as a problem of information, but in fact, as we have seen in section 2.5, people may be aware of their entitlement but not make a claim, as where they regard the status of recipient as stigmatizing. The problem of incomplete take-up is particularly associated with income-tested benefits, and is less serious for categorical benefits: for example, take-up of One Parent Benefit in the United Kingdom for 1984 was estimated at 93 per cent (H.M. Treasury, 1988, p. 273). As far as verification is concerned, the problem faced by the government in the case of income-testing is similar to that with tax evasion. As has been extensively discussed in the literature on evasion (see, for example, Cowell, 1990), the government has to decide on an audit policy (the proportion of claims investigated, and extent of the investigation, etc.) and on the structure of penalties imposed in the event of income being under-stated. The factors limiting the enforcement activity will obviously include its cost, but may also include the impact on the probability of claiming.

The problems of administration are illustrated by the Family Income Supplement (FIS) in the United Kingdom, the introduction of which involved devising new administrative procedures to collect relatively current income information (and Family Credit, which has since replaced it, requires in addition information on capital assets). The benefit must be claimed and would-be recipients have to supply information on income in the past five weeks or two months. This has imposed burdens on employers and potential claimants may have been deterred by the need to ask their employers for documentation.

[132]

Special procedures are necessary for the self-employed. An important simplification has been that, once the benefit has been assessed, no change in the payment is made for a specified period (which has been six months or one year). This means that the benefit paid is not necessarily appropriate to the current income, but reduces the administrative costs. Nonetheless, the administrative costs are significantly higher than those for the universal child benefit: 5.3 per cent of benefit expenditure, compared with 2.2 per cent for child benefit (Department of Social Security, 1993b, p. 20).

The calculation of benefits on the basis of past income is a device widely used in the administration of income-tested benefits. In France, certain benefits are based on net taxable income in the preceding tax year, so that applicants must make an annual declaration to the fiscal authorities, including those below the tax threshold who can obtain a certificate that they are not liable for income taxation. This considerably simplifies the administrative procedure. It does, however, entail adopting the income tax definitions in assessing benefit eligibility, and these may not be considered appropriate. The use of a past earnings period also means that there are inevitably people currently in receipt who are not eligible on the basis of current circumstances. An interview study in the United Kingdom by the Department of Health and Social Security (1975) found that over half of FIS recipients would have been entitled to less benefit if assessed at the date of interview and that 20 per cent would have had no entitlement. With an assessment based on income tax declarations, as in France, the problem is that receipt may be delayed far beyond the period of current need. A person whose income falls below the level of eligibility in tax year t may not be eligible in year $(t + 1)$, since the total annual income may exceed the ceiling, and have to wait until well into year $(t + 2)$.

Administrative obstacles are often disregarded by economists, who concentrate solely on the benefit schedule. However, in the case of income-tested transfers, it is very unlikely that the necessary information is available automatically to the government. Imperfect information may mean that some people receive benefits who are not entitled and that some of those entitled do not claim. This reduces the effectiveness of the income targeted transfer relative to a uniform benefit (see, for example, Besley, 1990).

Work disincentives

One of the most potent arguments in favour of targeting is that it reduces the total social security bill and hence the taxes which have to be levied on the rest of the population. Work disincentives are, it is argued, reduced for those financing the transfers. The significance of work disincentives can be over-stated, but in any case involve a trade-off. Lower taxes on the rest of the population are achieved at the expense of the very high marginal rates of tax which are implicit in the typical means-tested scheme. This is evident with the minimum income guarantee, involving a 100 per cent marginal tax rate, but other programmes, with more gradual tapers, may combine to create the same kind of 'poverty trap'.

In the United Kingdom, people on low income face the cumulation of several marginal tax rates. A person increasing his or her gross earnings pays higher income tax and National Insurance contributions. In 1992/3, the marginal tax rate over the relevant earnings range was 34 per cent, so that there remained in net terms a proportion $(1-0.34)$. For the low-paid family receiving Family Credit (FC) there would in addition be the withdrawal of means-tested benefits at the rate of 70 per cent of the additional net income when this is reassessed,[7] so that the net gain became $(1-0.34)(1-0.7) = 0.20$. If the person is also eligible for Community Charge Benefit (rebate on local tax), which is also means-tested and withdrawn at the rate of 15 per cent, and for Housing Benefit withdrawn at rate 65 per cent, the net gain becomes $(1-0.34)(1-0.7)(1-0.15-0.65) = 0.04$ (the calculations have been rounded to two figures). This structure of means-tests, applied to net income and taking into account benefits earlier in the chain, ensures that the overall marginal tax rate cannot exceed 100 per cent, but it reaches 96 per cent where all three benefits are received. As a result, the budget line relating net income to gross income is virtually flat for a wide band of earnings.

The position is further complicated by the aggregation of family earnings. The calculation in the previous paragraph assumes that there is only a single earner in the family, an assumption which does not apply in many cases and which fails to draw attention to the implications of means-tested benefits for family decisions. Since the test is applied to the joint earnings of husband and wife, they in effect face the same composite marginal tax rate as far as benefits are concerned. The situation is in this respect different from that which applies to income tax and National Insurance contributions, which are essentially operated on an individual basis. The poverty trap generated by means-tested benefits affects not just the main breadwinner but also his or her partner.

The conventional utility-maximizing model of labour supply predicts that a minimum income guarantee of amount g, with 100 per cent marginal tax rate, causes those with incomes below g to cease to

---

7 As explained earlier, benefit may be assessed on past income, which means that a rise in earnings may have no immediate impact on benefit receipt.

supply labour supply, and also affects a range of families whose incomes were previously above g. The size of the pre-transfer poverty population is increased. As a result, the cost of the transfer rises above the earlier calculation (although it may still be considerably less than that of a universal benefit). This is illustrated by the indirect utility function (3.4) considered earlier, according to which a person chooses not to work, but to live on the guaranteed income, g, where his previous income (assumed to be all earned) was less than $(1 + ,)$ times g. Since , is the elasticity of labour supply, we can see that the recipient population increases, other things equal, with the elasticity. A value of 0.5 means that the income-tested scheme brings in those whose incomes would otherwise be up to 50 per cent above the minimum income. In addition, the fact that recipients reduce their gross income to zero raises still further the cost of the transfer.

In order to see the implications of labour supply adjustments, let us take the earlier numerical example, but now assume that the wage rate (rather than income) is uniformly distributed over the relevant range upwards from zero. The proportion considered to be in poverty in the absence of transfers depends on whether we evaluate the position of individuals according to gross income or utility, as discussed in section 3.2. Suppose that we take gross income, so that those with

$$y = w\ell = w^{1+\beta} \leq \pi \tag{3.5}$$

are in poverty. With the poverty line at 50 per cent of average income, and H = 30 per cent as before, the poverty gap where $\beta = 0.5$ is equal to 9 per cent of total income.[8] If the available budget is a third of this gap, as before, then the transfer which can be financed is 32 per cent of the poverty line.[9] The reduction in the poverty gap is 20 per cent, compared with 10 per cent with a uniform transfer costing the same amount. The targeting advantage of the minimum income relative to a universal benefit is reduced when we take account

8 The headcount is given by the density times w^*, where w^* is the level of w such that (3.5) holds with equality. The poverty gap is

$(1 + \beta)/(2 + \beta) H\pi$.

9 The transfer is received by all those with w such that

$w^{1+\beta} \leq (1 + \beta) g$

If the budget is equal to t times the initial poverty gap, then the transfer which can be financed is

$g/\Pi = [t/(2 + \beta)]^{1+\beta/(2+\beta)} (1 + \beta)^{\beta/(2+\beta)}$

of the work disincentive. Of course, the comparison depends on the value of β and on the particular labour supply function,[10] but the calculation provides an indication of the possible importance.

Empirical evidence

Recent years have seen a great deal of research on the empirical magnitude of labour supply responses. In the reviews of this research there appears to be broad agreement that, to the extent that disincentive effects exist, they are modest in size.

In terms of hours of work, the value of 0.5 for the labour supply elasticity assumed in the numerical calculations is to the high end of the range typically estimated. The significance of labour supply adjustments may therefore be less than indicated. At the same time, labour supply has many dimensions. The main variations in annual hours may be attributable to periods out of the labour force (non-participation) or unemployment. While at work, people may be able to vary their effort, intensity of work, or the degree to which they are willing to take risks or responsibility. The working career has to be seen as a whole, with labour supply reductions taking the form of later entry or earlier retirement.

These dimensions of labour supply other than hours of work are important, because much less is known about how they are affected by transfer programmes. Even in principle the direction of the effect may be different. An income guarantee may give a positive incentive for people to make risky career decisions. Suppose that people are deciding whether or not to become self-employed, with all the attendant risks, rather than continue with a certain salary. The existence of an income supplement, payable in the event of low self-employment earnings, may induce them to take the plunge when they would not otherwise have been willing to do so. This would be further reinforced if the benefit served to finance an initial period of unprofitable operation before the business became successful.

A further possible disincentive, as we have seen, is that for the partners of the unemployed. If benefit is paid on a purely individual basis, then the marginal tax rate for the partner is zero, but where there is an income-test on family income the marginal rate may be 100 per cent. In the United Kingdom the participation rate of the wives of unemployed men is substantially lower than that of other married women, and this is especially true of those in receipt of

---

10 The function assumed here does not allow for any income effect on labour supply, whereas both the minimum income and the universal benefit may have income effects.

means-tested assistance (Dilnot and Kell, 1987). The estimates of Gregg and Wadsworth show that in 1993 the outflow rate from non-employment for women was 2H times as high where their partner was in work (1996, table 8.5). In the US in 1980 the unemployment rate for wives where the husband was unemployed was more than three times that where he was employed (*OECD*, 1982a, p. 35). There are a number of possible explanations for these patterns, and the disincentive of the family means-test is likely to explain only part of the difference, but it is an aspect which is often overlooked in the design of targeting. Where the unit of assessment is wider, then the same may apply to other household members.

The analysis of work incentives is further complicated by the fact that labour supply may not be purely the result of the decisions of individual workers. Choice of matters such as standard hours, or annual holiday, may be the result of collective bargaining. A transfer received by a minority of trade union members may have no impact on the collective choice. An individual worker is constrained by the labour market opportunities faced; the annual hours worked may be rationed where there is unemployment.

There are therefore grounds for being cautious about the conclusions which can be drawn regarding the relation between work incentives and the design of transfers. In fact, concern about incentives may arise as much from a notion of 'desert' as from the effect on labour supply, it being regarded as 'unfair' that a person is unable to improve materially his or her position by working more. If this is the case, then desert, rather than an equity-efficiency trade-off, may determine the maximum rate of withdrawal and hence the acceptable level of targeting.

Political economy

The problems which have been found in establishing an effective system of targeting – inadequate benefits, partial coverage, incomplete take-up, and the poverty trap – may appear to be matters of programme design. Given the resources, surely a safety net for the twenty-first century could be designed by people of goodwill? This is how it must have seemed to a succession of people and governments who have proposed plans for reform. Yet, these plans have come to little and the end results of reform have proved disappointing. More than 20 years ago, Henry Aaron (1973) was asking in the US, 'Why is welfare so hard to reform?' The answer appears to have much to do with the political economy of the welfare state.

The importance of political economy considerations is evident if we return to the analysis of targeting, in the previous section, which was predicated on a constant level of government spending. However, the total budget may not be independent of the form of transfer. Voters may be willing to support larger total expenditure on a universal programme than on a programme targeted to the poor. The ILO report *Into the Twenty-First Century* commented that the argument that:

> more generous provision could be made for the poor on an income-tested basis – seems at first sight to have a compelling logic. (International Labour Office, 1984, p. 23)

but went on to say that:

> people are more willing to contribute to a fund from which they derive benefit than to a fund going exclusively to the poor. The poor gain more from universal than from income-tested benefits. (1984, p. 23)

The choice of voters has been examined by De Donder and Hindriks (1996) in a simple median voter model. Holding the rate of withdrawal (*t* in our earlier analysis) constant, they consider voter preferences over different sized budgets. Starting from a low scale of programme, a voter may oppose any increase, but change his mind once the programme reaches a scale at which he benefits. Nonetheless, there is a level of the budget preferred by the median voter which is the majority voting equilibrium. In their formulation, this falls, rises and then falls as the degree of targeting (*t*) increases. The median voter withdraws support from the programme when he or she ceases to benefit. (When they allow both the budget and the rate of withdrawal to vary, they show that there may be no voting equilibrium such that one policy defeats all others in a pairwise majority vote.)

The formulation described above assumed that voters are only interested in their direct benefits, but there may be other motives, including a desire to help those with low incomes. These motives may favour greater targeting. For example, it could be argued that 'inefficient' targeting has been one of the grounds for political unwillingness to raise benefits and that demonstration of greater 'cost-effectiveness' would serve to increase the total budget. In order to explore this, we need to look in greater depth at the motives for supporting benefit transfers. At one extreme, there are the calls from the 'New Right' for a 'minimal' welfare state. A standard reference is Friedrich Hayek's *The Constitution of Liberty*:

> In the Western world some provision for those threatened by the extremes of indigence or starvation due to circumstances beyond their

control has long been accepted as a duty of the community. . . . The
necessity of some such arrangement in an industrial society is unques-
tioned – be it only in the interest of those who require protection
against acts of desperation on the part of the needy. (1960, p. 285)

After arguing that this may require compulsory insurance, and the
intervention of the state to develop appropriate institutions, Hayek
goes on to say that:

> Up to this point the justification for the whole apparatus of 'social
> security' can probably be accepted by the most consistent defenders of
> liberty. . . . Such a program as has been described would involve some
> coercion, but only coercion intended to forestall greater coercion of
> the individual in the interests of others; and the argument for it rests
> as much on the desire of individuals to protect themselves against the
> consequences of the extreme misery of their fellows as on any wish to
> force individuals to provide more effectively for their own needs. (1960,
> p. 286)

There are several possible interpretations of this position. Concern
with the 'extreme misery of their fellows' could refer to a sense of
solidarity, or, in welfare economic terms, that there is some level of
well-being, which if not achieved generates negative externalities. On
the other hand, the first quotation indicates a less charitable interpretation, where the concern is that of avoiding political unrest. The
legitimacy of the government in power may be questioned if the
disparities of income become too large.

A third interpretation of the passage from Hayek is that a national
minimum is justified as a means to securing individual freedom. As
Hayek recognizes, such an argument requires the balancing of different liberties; and the degree of agreement may be less than he indicates. This has been brought out in the debate about 'negative' and
'positive' concepts of freedom, the former concerned with the absence of restraints and the latter concerned with the presence of possibilities (see, for example, Sen, 1988). Many have argued that the
effective enjoyment of liberty, in political, legal and other spheres,
depends on the existence of a social minimum. But there are others
who hold that what liberty requires is the absence of interference
from others and this negative interpretation of freedom would regard legislated transfers as harmful to liberty. Considerations of liberty do not necessarily lead to a justification of the
minimal welfare state.

Moreover, amongst those who support a social minimum on grounds
of positive freedom, there are differences of view. As has been argued
by Goodin (1988), in order to understand the liberty argument more
fully, we need to provide more structure on the class of actors, the

[139]

nature of the constraints and the range of actions. In particular, we can distinguish, on the one hand, the argument that the welfare state increases the freedom of *recipients* from social and economic obstacles to live their lives, and, on the other hand, the increased freedom which it provides for *all citizens* from real or perceived constraints on their actions. It is the former position that is usually highlighted, but the latter is possibly important. The establishment of a social minimum is seen as allowing the citizen to pursue with a clear conscience other objectives such as economic growth and profit. This is illustrated by the account given of the French 'solidarist' movement by Tony Lynes, of which the aim was

> to liberate [private property] from the 'social debt' which its possessors owed to the less fortunate members of society. (1967, pp. 46–7)

It is again a question of legitimacy.

The political arguments are therefore more complex than may at first sight appear, and it is important to understand the motives which lie behind calls for greater targeting. These may lead in rather different directions from what initially appears to be tbe case.

3.4 Towards a European Minimum

In this section, I consider the case for action at the European level to secure a minimum income, and the form which such minimum provision should take. This is informed by the discussion in the preceding sections of the targeting of social transfer programmes, but first we need to consider the justification which can be given for a European policy.

Europe-wide social policy

In the early days of the European Community, social policy received relatively little attention, and the Community's organs were provided with very limited powers in the social field. Social policy was, to a large extent, a means towards achieving other objectives. The restructuring of the coal and steel industries, through the European Coal and Steel Community, involved social measures in aid of training and to finance adjustment. There was concern with removing barriers to labour mobility and ensuring that differences in the costs of social protection did not prevent competition in the supply of goods. In the 1970s the social dimension of the Community began to play a more important role. Some writers (Crijns, 1991) attribute this in part to the debates which took place about the social aspect while the United Kingdom and others were deciding on accession to the Community. The issue was certainly raised by opponents of entry. Within the Community, the 1972 Paris Conference called for measures to reduce social and regional inequalities. In the social field, the Commission produced a Social Action Programme, accepted by the Council in 1974, which recognized that the Community had an independent role to play in the formation of social policy and among the measures agreed were:

1   To extend gradually social protection to cate-gories of people not covered or inadequately provided-for under existing schemes; and
2   To implement, in co-operation with Member States, specific measures to combat poverty.

In terms of concrete action, the achievements were limited in scale and scope. The Regional Development Fund was put in place. The Social Fund was increased in size, with an emphasis on the education, training and insertion into the labour market of young persons, and on regional redistribution. Policy to combat poverty led in July 1975 to the first European Action Programme covering the period 1975–80. In December 1981, the Commission made an evaluation report, containing the estimate of the number of poor people in the Community referred to in the Introduction to these Lectures. Despite the concern generated by these figures, it took several years to agree the Second Action Programme for the period 1985–9. This was followed by a third programme stressing social exclusion and marginalisation.

At the same time, the social dimension was receiving more attention generally in the Community. In 1989 the Commission put forward a draft of the 'Community Charter of Fundamental Social Rights' and this was adopted in modified form at the Strasbourg European Council in December 1989 by 11 of the 12 Member States (with the United Kingdom dissenting). For our purposes here, the key paragraph is number 10, which states that:

> Every worker of the European Community shall have a right to adequate social protection and shall, whatever his status and whatever the size of the undertaking in which he is employed, enjoy an adequate level of social security benefits.
>
> Persons who have been unable to enter or re-enter the labour market and have no means of subsistence must be able to receive sufficient resources and social assistance in keeping with their particular situation.

The opposition of the United Kingdom at the Maastricht European Council led to the Social Chapter being excluded from the final Treaty on European Union, but there was an attached Social Protocol, in which the other members expressed their wish to continue along the path laid down in the 1989 Social Charter, and their intention to take decisions outside the Treaty.

Subsidiarity

Whether or not there can be action at the European level depends on how far social protection is deemed to be within the competence of the European Union. This brings us to the principle of subsidiarity. Article 3b of the Treaty on European Union states that:

> the Community shall take action, in accordance with the principle of subsidiarity, only if and insofar as the objectives of the proposed action cannot be sufficiently achieved by the member states and can therefore, by reason of the scale or effects of the proposed action, be better achieved by the Community.

What, however, exactly does the principle of subsidiarity mean? In the public finance literature on decentralization, there has been analysis of the allocation of functions to different levels of government, particularly between federal (which I take to be the European Union in the present context) and local (which I take to be the national governments of the Member States). Some have argued that functions should be allocated to local governments where there are marked differences in preferences between local areas. As James Meade has put it in his paper on 'The Building of a New Europe' (1991), this allows freedom for *national diversity*, as opposed to *continental uniformity*. This criterion has been applied by Pauly (1973) in which he describes redistribution as a local public good. Subsidiarity would then mean that a Member State was free to determine the extent of redistribution on the basis of the expressed preferences of its electorate. Some countries would choose a highly redistributive policy, with associated higher taxes, and others would provide less social protection. This is not, however, what is envisaged in Article 3b, which refers explicitly to *the objectives of the proposed action*. In other words, it does not leave the lower-level government free to determine the *objectives* of redistributive policy. While the Social Charter is consistent with Country A pursuing more than average egalitarian policies, it presumes that there is agreement on a minimum level of social protection that even country B is required to provide.

This interpretation is supported by reference to the principle of subsidiarity in Catholic social doctrine, which applied this principle long before the European Community was invented.[11] The Catholic principle is surely based on assumed agreement about basic objectives. It is not a question of the Catholic Church handing over moral authority to lower levels of organisation. Moreover, it emphasizes the role of the central authority in *supporting* the activities of the lower level bodies. In accordance with the generally 'corporatist' aims of Pius XI, the central authority was seen to have the role of providing aid to lower levels in a mutual attempt to achieve common goals. As it was put by the American Bishops:

> Government should not replace or destroy smaller communities and individual initiative. Rather it should help them to contribute more effectively to social well-being and supplement their activity when the demands of justice exceed their capacities. (1986, para 124, cited in Gannon, 1987)

So that, while subsidiarity undoubtedly means different things to different people, one reasonable interpretation is that the European Union should act to support the social protection activities of Member States and to fill the gaps at the national level. The Union should 'supplement' their activity when the demands of justice exceed their capacities.

The capacities of Member States to combat poverty are indeed under threat. This argument has been made forcefully by Hans-Werner Sinn:

> the poor will lose because governments will no longer be able to maintain their current scales of redistribution. . . . it will be difficult for a single country to extract the required funds from the rich. On the other hand, net benefits being given to the poor in one jurisdiction will attract poor people from everywhere and so make this policy unsustainable. The New York city effect will be the death of Europe's welfare states if the unmitigated competition of tax systems is allowed. (1990, pp. 501–2)

Such a contention suggests that the national governments may indeed be in need of Union assistance in ensuring adequate social protection. There are however two aspects which we need to clarify. The first is that Sinn's argument does not apply equally to all forms of social security provision. If we take a *social insurance* scheme, and if we abstract from problems of asymmetric information, then the provision of actuarially fair unemployment or retirement insurance is val-

11 The classic reference is the encyclical Quadragesimo Anno (On Reconstructing the Social Order) of Pius XI, published in 1931; see also such documents as the 1986 Letter of the American Catholic Bishops.

ued by risk-averse workers, and will be reflected in the wages demanded. Where social insurance furnishes a transparent link between contributions and benefits, then it is less subject to the downward pressures of fiscal competition. The contribution principle is at least a partial defence against competitive pressures to dismantle the welfare state. What one has to look at is the *net benefit* from the social insurance scheme, and this may well make countries with high levels of social protection attractive to prospective workers. High social contributions may not be a deterrent if they are matched by comparable benefits. Of course, it is possible that a scheme which is actuarily fair over a person's lifetime nonetheless involves periods when it is advantageous to opt out. It is, however, clear that the main problem arises with the *redistributive* elements of social protection. Since much of social security is not in fact redistributive, at least on a life-cycle perspective, this limits the applicability of his fiscal competition argument. At the same time, the argument applies with particular force to anti-poverty policies. National governments will be under pressure to reduce transfers to the poor.

The second question concerns the mechanism by which this pressure will be exerted on national governments. It is important to distinguish different forms of reaction. Sinn refers principally to the migration of labour, but there are reasons to doubt whether this will be of sufficient quantitative importance, at least in the foreseeable future. The evidence from the US about 'welfare migration' between states with different levels of benefits (for example, Peterson and Rom (1990)) suggests that there is a significant effect, but that its quantitative magnitude is rather small. If we turn to the effect on contributors, rather than beneficiaries, then the evidence for the European Union to date does not suggest that substantial migration has been induced by the significant differences which exist between member states in net of tax wage rates. Ermisch after examining the evidence for different countries noted:

> the failure of the pattern or volume of migration among EC countries
> to change much after the formation of the EC. (Ermisch, 1991, p. 101)

The mechanism may, however, be a different one from labour migration. It may be the location decisions of firms and investment policies that are affected. The European Commission has warned that there may be what it calls 'social dumping', whereby the countries with the lowest levels of benefits attract businesses, via lower labour costs, and this puts those with more generous welfare provisions at a competitive disadvantage. This argument, as noted above, does not apply where the welfare provisions provide a net benefit, but it may apply to redistributive social assistance. The United Kingdom, by not signing the Social Charter, and by holding down the level of social assistance, sought to increase domestic employment. It is not clear that there is a great deal of empirical evidence to support this position, and it is easy to imagine arguments in the reverse direction. If companies are not myopic, but are deciding on a location for the medium-term, then they will foresee that such a policy may provoke reactions, either along the Sinn lines, or through barriers erected against a country not accepting the social provisions.

There remains, however, a further dimension to the argument – and perhaps the most important. Rather than real tax competition, there may be *virtual* tax competition, based on potential or threatened, movement of labour or capital. Hirschman (1970) distinguished between 'exit' and 'voice' as reactions to economic change. Workers, or companies, who perceive that taxes are lower in other member states may not migrate but may seek to exercise political power, or voice, to achieve lower taxes at home. Comparisons of tax rates with those in other member countries will play a role in national election campaigns. In a world where the presentation of policy, and its reception by markets and the media, are seen to be of paramount importance, it may well be that the perceived pressures of virtual tax competition become the most important restrictions on the freedom of national governments to carry out social protection. A Europe-wide anti-poverty policy can be justified on these 'political economy' grounds.

3.5 What Form for a European Minimum?

If a social dimension to the Union is to develop alongside the Internal Market and the Monetary Union, if we are to meet a European poverty target, then what form should the European minimum take? It seems that the Social Charter has in mind in the second part of paragraph 10, a form of income-tested social assistance. Beyond this, what precisely the paragraph means is not entirely clear. A senior official of the Commission described the clauses on social protection in the following terms:

> They are very open-ended and are stated in very general terms, because the concept of 'sufficient resources' remains to be determined. (Quintin, 1989, p. 4)

For the reasons given earlier in this Lecture, I do not consider means-testing the way forward. The means-tested approach penalizes personal effort with marginal tax rates higher than those levied on the rest of the population. The effect at the level of the individual worker may not quantitatively be large, but it offends notions of fairness. In terms of work effort, it is not just individual efforts that are penalized, but those of the person's family. Unlike individualized social insurance, social assistance discourages the partners of those out of work from earning income. The popular objection to means-tested benefits is revealed in the recurrent problem of incomplete take-up. A significant minority of those with incomes below the assistance level do not claim the benefits to which they are entitled. Some may welcome this as a sign of independence but liberation from the state may not mean self-sufficiency but dependence on others. Adult children may be dependent on their parents; elderly parents may be dependent on their children; women may have to stay with abusing partners. The means-test itself can only make sense when applied to the family or the household as a unit. As such, it runs counter to the desire to have a social security system which ensures independence.

Britain has the dubious advantage that it has experimented extensively with means-tested social assistance, and we have seen its shortcomings. The saying of Santayana that those who do not remember the past are condemned to repeat it, should perhaps be extended to include to those who do not learn from the experience of their neighbours. This applies with even more force if we look ahead to the ways in which European policy may be aligned. The definition of a social minimum is a complex matter, and the complexity is much greater for an income-tested scheme. This has many dimensions, and if we ask whether a particular Member State is providing the agreed minimum level of social protection, then this is not easily verified. If we are seeking a basis for the second-tier which allows a European-wide, and not just a national, minimum to be set in place, then it has to be based on a benefit which is simpler in structure than means-tested social assistance.

In my view, we need to combine elements of old and new. 'Old' in the form of social insurance, which is the backbone of the social transfer system in all European countries; 'new' in the form of a conditional basic income, which I refer to as a Participation Income. Social insurance, which provides benefits to people as individuals without tests of means, enjoys considerable public support, including the confidence of the social partners. Diversity can be accommodated, with appropriate provision for those working in more than one country. Social insurance, as argued above, is less subject to the pressures of fiscal competition, and can continue to be operated at a national level.

There are, at the same time, limitations to social insurance. There are gaps in coverage. Social insurance, which had its origins in the modern employment relationship, does not always recognize the needs of those outside the formal economy, such as people taking care of dependent relatives. It may exclude those who have not had labour market attachment, such as those disabled from birth, or young people entering the labour market for the first time, or mothers returning to work when their children have ceased to be dependent. There may be difficulties in providing for part-time employees and for the more flexible working arrangements that are likely to characterize the twenty-first century. It cannot readily allow for people opting out of the formal employment status for significant periods of their lives, pursuing some alternative life-style. (The significance of these problems varies from country to country.)

The limitations of social insurance are one reason why the idea of a basic income, or citizen's income, has been put forward as an alternative. In its pure form, the basic income would replace all existing social insurance and assistance benefits by a single payment, paid on an individual basis, without any test of means, and paid unconditionally. The benefit would also replace all income tax allowances, and in this sense there would be an integration of taxation and social security, although the tax would be collected in a separate operation. In the simplest form of the scheme, there would be a single tax rate on all income.

In my view, however, it is a mistake to see basic income as an *alternative* to social insurance. There remains strong support for social insurance, not least among the social partners who are influential in a European context. Moreover, this support is not without foundation. The differentiation involved in the typical social insurance scheme is not arbitrary, and the citizen's income payments would need to retain some categorical elements. The relation of benefits received to contributions paid reduces the risk of fiscal competition between governments in the European Union.

It is more productive to see basic income as complementary to social insurance. For this reason, I am much more persuaded by the approach to basic income adopted in the United Kingdom by Hermione Parker (1989). She outlines a scheme that would replace tax allowances, although retaining an earned income, but would keep the existing structure of social insurance benefits. She regards this as the first phase of a move to a basic income, but I would see this partnership between social insurance and basic income not just as a transitional compromise, but as an alternative conception of the basic income.

But this is not enough to ensure political support. It is noteworthy that, despite the attention which basic income been given, and despite finding supporters in all political parties, the scheme has not got close to being introduced. If one asks why, then, in my judgement a major reason for opposition to basic income lies in its lack of conditionality. There are concerns that it will lead to dependency, or state-induced social exclusion. I believe therefore that, in order to secure political support, it may be necessary for the proponents of basic income to compromise – not on the principle of no test of means, nor on the principle of independence, but on the unconditional payment. In terms of the question posed by Phillipe Van Parijs (1991) – Would we pay basic income to surfers? – my answer is 'no'.

A participation income

The above arguments lead me to support a basic income conditional on *participation*. The way in which this participation would be defined requires detailed consideration. The qualifying conditions for adults would no doubt include (a) work as an employee or self-employed, (b) absence from work on grounds of sickness, injury, or disability, (c) being unemployed but available for work, (d) reaching pension age, (e) engaging in approved forms of education or training, and (f) caring for young, elderly or disabled dependents (there would in addition be a basic income for children, such as child benefit). As the last examples make clear, the condition is not *paid* work; it is a wider definition of social contribution. The determination of these conditions would undoubtedly involve problems, problems which would not arise with the unconditional basic income. And these problems would mean that there were people who failed to secure the basic income.[12] There would undoubtedly be behavioural responses, as people adjusted their actions in order to qualify. On the other hand, these adjustments would be in the direction of social inclusion.

The participation condition would help meet one of the objections to a basic income, which is that it would mean making payments to people who currently enjoy sizeable incomes but pay no income tax: for example, self-employed people who are not declaring their earnings. With the extension of the tax to all income, and the increase in the tax rate necessary to finance the basic income, this would become a more serious problem. The participation prerequisite would require such people to declare their professional status as a condition of receiving the basic income. While this would not ensure full declaration, it would provide a basis on which the tax authorities could monitor self-employment activity. There would be a degree of accountability which would not be present with an unconditional basic income.

There are undoubtedly potential problems with the Participation

12 There would therefore need to be a residual means-tested safety net, but its role would be limited.

Income. Its effectiveness in preventing poverty depends on the level at which it would be set. The basic payment would be more visible than social assistance and there are those who argue that it would be more vulnerable to benefit cuts by a national government. (I have discussed the public choice aspects of a basic income in Atkinson (1995).) The issue of benefit level would arise still more acutely if the Participation Income were instituted at a European-level, and there would be the problem of the interpretation of the participation condition in different contexts. There are evident common elements with the concept of 'insertion' embodied in the French *Revenu Minimum d'Insertion*, but these would need to be developed in the details of legislation and administrative practice.

I believe that such a Participation Income offers a realistic way in which European governments may be persuaded that a basic income offers a better route forward than the dead end of means-tested assistance. New ideas in this field are needed, and this one combines the twin concerns with poverty and with social exclusion that have been one of the main themes of these Lectures.

Envoi

Poverty, Policy and
Mainstream Economics

The aim of these Lectures has to been to illuminate the extent of poverty in Europe and the economic causes that lie behind the persistence of concern about poverty in rich countries.

How much poverty there is in Europe, and how it is changing over time, are questions which can only be answered by posing still further questions. Where do we draw the poverty line? Is it absolute or relative? Should we look at expenditure or at income? How should we allow for the differing needs of different families? How should we measure poverty? The first Lecture has attempted to address these conceptual issues. Its title echoed the seventeenth-century *Political Arithmetick* by Sir William Petty, of whom Phyllis Deane has written that:

> he was not above manipulating his data in ways that would justify his polemical arguments. (*International Encyclopedia of the Social Sciences*, vol. 12, p. 67)

At the same time, in his Preface, Petty was delightfully open in expressing the hope that:

> all ingenious and candid persons will rectify the Errors, Defects and Imperfections which probably may be found. (1676, p. x in 1964 edition)

It is because of the highly political role of poverty statistics that it is essential that their conceptual and statistical basis should be subject to careful – and independent – scrutiny. This in turn means that it is important that the raw statistical materials, the micro-data from household surveys, be accessible to outside researchers at a reasonable

[150]

price. Eurostat has done an extraordinarily good job, with the aid of national statistical agencies, in commencing work in this area. They deserve credit for what has been done and for the initiatives planned at present. But it is vital that this be accompanied by independent research. Given the sensitivity of the findings to the methods employed, and to the choice of definitions, it is imperative that the conclusions be open to outside scrutiny.

The second Lecture turned to the role of economic analysis in the study of poverty. When I first studied economics, there were very few economists working on distributional issues in general, let alone on the subject of poverty. Then in the mid-1960s it became a fashionable subject, with the launching of the War on Poverty in the United States, but even so it was not really central to the concerns of the economics profession, and this has remained the case. The subject of the distribution of income has been marginalized in mainstream economics. This means that we lack an adequate economic framework to understand the causes of poverty, and that the objective of alleviating poverty is not integrated within the standard accounts of economic policy-making. At the same time, there are promising directions of research, as I have tried to demonstrate. Economic analysis can illuminate the meaning of poverty, and its relation to social exclusion. It can sharpen the questions which we ask, as well as offering some answers.

Policy towards the elimination of poverty has been the subject of Lecture 3. Here we need to understand not only the reforms which are necessary but also the political economy of anti-poverty policy. I have argued that the institution of an official poverty target can have a substantive effect on policy outcomes, and I have elsewhere (Atkinson, 1996) made the case for an official Poverty Target and Report in the United Kingdom, parallel to the Inflation Target and Report. One important argument in favour of a poverty target is that it would place anti-poverty policy on the same footing as macro-economic policy. A poverty target would allow those concerned about poverty to compete for public attention on more equal terms with other objectives such as economic growth or price stability.

We cannot consider anti-poverty policy in isolation from other policies. The scope for financing income maintenance depends on macro-economic policy choices, on levels of government spending, and on rates of inflation. The use of transfer payments, or other instruments of anti-poverty policy, such as education and training or health care, in turn have implications for economic policy. Social and economic policy are interdependent. This may appear obvious, but it remains the case that social policy is often placed in a separate compartment. Economic policy tends to have first claim on our attention, with social policy accommodating to the results. This is alarming

[151]

not just because of the interdependence, but also because it appears that undue faith is placed in the efficacy of social policy to solve the distributional problems generated by macro-economic policy. As we have seen, the popular recommendation of greater targeting of social transfers is less promising than appears at first sight. We have to search for new approaches, particularly at the European level. The way forward, in my view, is in (reformed) social insurance at the national level, coupled with a Participation Income to provide a European minimum.

Finally, as we think about developments in Europe, we should not lose sight of the objective of eliminating world poverty, which in my view has precedence. There are two aspects of these Lectures which have some relevance here. First, the comments about the neglect of distributional issues in mainstream economics apply also to the neglect of the world distribution. Second, the constraints on the scale of assistance to poor countries are, in my judgement, more political than budgetary. A society which is concerned about the situation of its least fortunate members is also more likely to be generous in aiding poor countries – Scandinavia being an obvious example – and that is one reason why it was a pleasure to give these Lectures in Helsinki.

Appendix on Statistical Sources

This appendix provides a brief description of the statistical sources.

European Community

The study by Hagenaars et al. (1994)[1] was the first to make use of micro-data from the household budget surveys of all twelve member states supplied to Eurostat. Corrections were made to the data by the investigators to allow for differences in definitions and methodology. Household weights were applied to improve the representativeness of the surveys. Total household expenditure is defined to include all household expenditure except mortgage payments plus imputed rent for owner-occupied dwellings,[2] self-supplied goods and income in kind. The head of the household is defined as the person who brings in the largest share of total household resources.

In the 1990s, Eurostat launched the new European Community Household Panel Survey (ECHP), which is a most important development. It is a multi-dimensional survey covering income, education, labour force status, housing and other household characteristics. Fieldwork, which is carried out by national contractors, yielded a sample of some 61,100 households in Wave 1 of the ECHP. This was carried out in 1994 and provided information about incomes in 1993. These data were used by Eurostat (1997) in their estimates of income poverty for 1993.

1 See also de Vos and Zaidi (1995, 1995a).
2 Imputed rent is included in the survey data for all countries except Denmark (where it has been calculated as 2.5 per cent of the value of the house) and France (estimated using a regression of rent for tenant households).

[153]

Luxembourg Income Study

An important source of data for cross-country comparisons is the Luxembourg Income Study (LIS). The LIS database contains micro-data from a wide range of household surveys in different countries and covering different periods. (See Atkinson, Rainwater and Smeeding, 1995, for further information.) The LIS data have been used for cross-country comparisons of poverty by, among others, Förster (1994), Bradshaw and Chen (1996), and Van den Bosch (1996).

Belgium

In Belgium, there is a household budget survey (Enquête sur les Budgets des Ménages), which was used for the study by Hagenaars et al. (1994). The survey is carried out at intervals (for example, 1987–8) by the national statistical agency. It covers a representative sample of about 3,000 Belgian households, who are required to complete a booklet in which all expenditure and income are recorded for a year. The sample is re-weighted by a system of weights based on region, socio-professional category and household size.

A second source of evidence about income poverty in Belgium is the CSP panel survey, which covers all private households in Belgium. It was carried out in 1985 (first wave), in 1988 (second wave) and in 1992. The number of households interviewed is about 4,000. The enquiry obtains information about the income received during the month previous to the interview and about other characteristics of the household. There is no expenditure information. For a discussion of the coverage of investment income, see Meulemans and Marannes (1993). Cantillon (1992) reports data from the CSP survey covering the *Flemish population* for 1976, 1982 and 1985.

Finland

The source for the years 1976, 1981, 1985 and 1990 is the household budget survey, which is a sample survey carried out at approximately five-year intervals. There is a response rate of about 70 per cent and around 8,000 responding households (in 1985). The responses are re-weighted to correct for the biases due to non-response (Uusitalo, 1989, p. 28). In addition to the data collected from households, information on incomes, taxes and transfers is derived from administrative records, such as those of the Social Insurance Institution. The data for 1991, 1992 and 1993 are taken from the income distribution statistics.

France

In France, two major sources have been used to assess the extent of low incomes.[3] The first is the Enquête sur les Revenus Fiscaux (ERF), based on income tax declarations. The ERF proceeds by drawing a sample of households and matching the households with income tax declarations; this is achieved in 85 per cent of cases, with corrections being applied in other cases. A re-weighting process is then applied, based on occupational category and size of commune. Part of nontaxable income (family benefits, *minimum-vieillesse*, *revenu minimum d'insertion* (RMI)) is incorporated by an imputation procedure: i.e. attributing to each household its calculated entitlement, not allowing for incomplete take-up.

The second source in France is that used in section 1.1: the household budget survey, the *Enquête sur les Budgets Familiaux* (EBF). The EBF is conducted periodically and collects information by interview on expenditure, income and other variables. To adjust for differential non-response between different types of household in the French EBF, a grossing-up procedure is applied to yield results representative of the population. The surveys for 1979, 1984–5 and 1989 were intended to collect information about current income; the 1995 survey measured annual income in the twelve months preceding the interview.

Germany

Two main sample surveys have been used in the study of poverty in West Germany (to which attention is limited here).[4] The first is the *Einkommens- und Verbrauchstichprobe* (EVS), which is the official household budget survey and is conducted periodically. It collects information by interview and diaries on expenditure, income and other variables. The survey is unusual in that it is not based on a random sample but on a call for volunteers. To adjust for differential non-response between different types of household a re-weighting procedure is applied. It also excludes all households with a non-German head (in the years before 1993). The data available to Becker (1996) excluded, for data protection reasons, households con-

3 For a more general discussion of the statistical sources on poverty in France and their limitations, see for example Faure (1989) and CERC (1989, pp. 101–2). Further references are contained in Déchaux (1990).
4 For a fuller discussion of the different sources of evidence about poverty in Germany, see Hauser and Semrau (1990).

seven or more persons, and excluded high income households (in 1993 above 35,000 DM monthly net income).

The second main source is the Socio-Economic Panel (GSOEP), which is a longitudinal survey, representative of the household population, including those with non-German heads. The first wave was conducted in 1984. The survey was extended to the East German *Länder* in 1990. The survey collects information by interview on income and other variables. The results are grossed up using weights from the Microcensus.

Ireland

The Household Budget Survey (HBS) is carried out periodically by the Central Statistics Office. It is primarily an expenditure survey but contains detailed income data (a description of the HBS is given in Murphy (1984)). The results are reweighted to adjust for differential non-response.

A separate household survey, the Survey of Income Distribution, Poverty and Use of State Services, was carried out by the Economic and Social Research Institute (ESRI) in 1987. This is described in Callan et al. (1989, ch. 4). The ESRI survey contained detailed questions on income, non-cash benefits received, and on styles of living. A re-weighting scheme is applied based on household location, number of adults, occupation and age of household head. It was found necessary to take special account of the problems in measuring farm income, on account of the relatively high proportion engaged in this sector, and this was covered by a special questionnaire.

Income distribution data for 1994 were collected in the 1994 Living in Ireland Survey, which was the first wave of the European Community Household Panel in Ireland. The survey is described in Callan et al. (1996) and Nolan (1996). In the 1994 survey, additional information was obtained in order to allow income to be measured on the same basis as in the 1987 survey. The survey covers private households in Ireland. The target sample, excluding invalid elements, was 7,086 households, and the overall response rate 57.1 per cent, yielding an interview total of 4,048 households containing 14,583 persons. The results were re-weighted to allow for differential non-response. A special farm questionnaire was used to estimate farm incomes.

Italy

There are two main national sources of income and expenditure data in Italy.[5] The first is the Bank of Italy sample survey of households,

5 These two sources are described in detail by Brandolini (1993).

in which families are interviewed about their income in the preceding calendar year. The definition of income has been modified over the years, but the Bank of Italy has constructed a historical dataset from 1977 which secures the greatest possible degree of temporal consistency. There is a post-stratification re-weighting of family units, to correct for differential response rates by sampling stratum.

The second source is the Istat survey of family budgets, which was extended in 1979 to include questions on family monthly income. The institutional population is excluded. It is primarily an expenditure survey but interviewees are asked to provide an estimate of the total after-tax income earned in a month by all members of the family. This is a single question, and the lack of a specific reference month means that seasonal variations, and thirteen-month bonuses, may be omitted. The accuracy is also reduced by the fact that families are asked to respond in terms of 16 prearranged income classes. The Istat control procedure eliminates those families whose expenditure appears to be unreasonably low compared with similar families in the same area.

Netherlands

There are two main sources. The first is the annual budget survey (Budgetonderzoek) carried out by Statistics Netherlands and covering some 2,000 households.

The second source is the Socio-Economic Panel (SEP) is a household panel survey, of which the first wave was in April 1984. It was carried out in April and October of each year until April 1990, when it became annual. It contains information on about 5,000 households with 13,000 individuals. To correct for initial non-response and subsequent attrition, households are added and the respondents are re-weighted.

Sweden

The source used by the Swedish Ministry of Finance (1996) is the household income distribution survey (HINK), which is a rotating sample of about 13,000 households, with a response rate of about 80 per cent. In addition to the data collected from households, information on incomes, taxes and transfers is derived from administrative records.

United Kingdom

In the United Kingdom, the main source that has been used to date to measure income poverty is the Family Expenditure Survey (FES).

The primary purpose of the FES is to collect the expenditure information necessary to construct the weights for the Retail Prices Index, but it also collects a substantial quantity of income data. The FES is a representative sample of private households in the United Kingdom. The sample size for Great Britain is about 10,000, the sample being drawn each year (there is no panel element). The institutional population is excluded. The response rate in 1994/5 was 66 per cent, giving a total of 6,730 responding households. The primary reason for non-response (31 per cent) was refusal to co-operate. In order to adjust for differential non-response, differential grossing-up weights are applied in a number of studies.

Recently, the Households Below Average Income series (for example, Department of Social Security, 1996), based on the FES, has made use of aggregate data on very high incomes from the SPI, which is based on a sample survey by the Inland Revenue of income tax declarations and which is restricted to those people for whom income tax records are held. The reason for making the SPI adjustment is to arrive at more accurate estimates of mean incomes (see Department of Social Security, 1991).

References

Aaron, H. J., 1973, *Why is Welfare So Hard to Reform?*, Washington, D.C.: Brookings Institution.

Abel-Smith, B., and Townsend, P., 1965, *The Poor and the Poorest*, London: Bell.

Alesina, A., 1988, 'Credibility and Policy Convergence in a Two-Party System with Rational Voters', *American Economic Review*, vol. 78, pp. 796–805.

Amiel, Y. and Cowell, F. A., 1996, 'Distributional Orderings and the Transfer Principle: A re-examination', Distributional Analysis Research Programme, Discussion Paper 14, London School of Economics.

Anand, S. and Ravallion, M., 1993, 'Human Development in Poor Countries: On the Role of Private Incomes and Public Services', *Journal of Economic Perspectives*, vol. 7, no. 133–50.

Assémat, J. and Glaude, M., 1989, 'Source fiscale et/ou enquête par interview: l'experience française en matière de mesure des bas revenus', Noordwijk: paper presented at Eurostat Conference.

Atkinson, A. B., 1969, *Poverty in Britain and the Reform of Social Security*, Cambridge: Cambridge University Press.

——, 1970, 'On the measurement of inequality', *Journal of Economic Theory*, vol. 2, 244–63.

——, 1983, *The Economics of Inequality*, second edition, Oxford: Clarendon Press.

——, A. B., 1987, 'On the Measurement of Poverty', *Econometrica*, vol. 55, 749–64.

——, 1989, *Poverty and Social Security*, Hemel Hempstead: Harvester Wheatsheaf.

——, 1990, 'Poverty, statistics and progress in Europe', *Analyzing Poverty in the European Community*, Luxembourg: Eurostat News

Special Edition, 1–1990.

——, 1995, *Public Economics in Action: The Basic Income/Flat Tax Proposal*, Oxford: Oxford University Press.

——, 1995a, 'Capabilities, exclusion, and the supply of goods' in K. Basu, P. Pattanaik and K. Suzumura (eds), *Choice, Welfare, and Development*, Oxford: Clarendon Press.

——, 1996, 'Promise and performance: Why we need an official poverty report' in P. Barker (ed.), *Living as Equals*, Oxford: Oxford University Press.

——, 1997, 'Bringing Income Distribution in from the Cold', *Economic Journal*, vol. 107, 297–321.

——, forthcoming, *The Economic Consequences of Rolling Back the Welfare State*, Cambridge, Massachusetts: MIT Press.

——, Blanchard, O. J., Fitoussi, J.-P., Flemming, J. S., Malinvaud, E., Phelps, E. S. and Solow, R. M., 1994, *Pour l'emploi et la Cohésion Sociale*, Paris: Presses de la Fondation Nationale des Science Politiques.

—— and Cazes, S., 1990, 'Mesures de la pauvreté et politiques sociales', *Observations et Diagnostics Economiques, Revue de l'OFCE*, vol. 33, 105–30.

—— and Champion, B., 1989, 'Family income supplement and two-parent families, 1971–1980', in Atkinson, A. B., 1989, *Poverty and Social Security*, Hemel Hempstead: Harvester Wheatsheaf.

——, Gardiner, K., Lechene, V. and Sutherland, H, 1993, 'Comparing Poverty in France and the United Kingdom', Welfare State Programme Discussion Paper 84, LSE.

—— and Micklewright, J., 1991, 'Unemployment compensation and labor market transitions: a critical review', *Journal of Economic Literature*, vol. 29, 1679–727.

——, Rainwater, L., and Smeeding, T., 1995, *Income Distribution in OECD Countries*, Paris: OECD.

Balestrino, A., 1994, 'Poverty and Functionings: Issues in Measurement and Public Action', *Giornale degli Economiste e Annali di Economia*, vol. 53, 389–406.

——, 1996, 'A Note on Functioning-Poverty in Affluent Societies', *Notizie di Politeia*, vol. 12, 97–105.

Banks, J. and Johnson, P., 1994, 'Equivalence scale relativities revisited', *Economic Journal*, vol. 104, 883–90.

Bean, C. R., 1994, 'European unemployment: a survey', *Journal of Economic Literature*, vol. 32, 573–619.

Becker, G. S., 1965, 'A Theory of the Allocation of Time', *Economic Journal*, vol. 75, 493–517.

Becker, I., 1996, 'Die Entwicklung der Einkommen-sverteilung und der Einkommensarmut in den alten Bundesländern von 1962 bis 1988' in Becker, I. and Hauser, R., 1996, 'Einkommensverteilung und Armut in Deutschland von 1962 bis 1995', Arbeitspapier Nr 9, Universität Frankfurt am Main: EVS-Projekt.

Beckerman, W., 1979, 'The impact of income maintenance payments on poverty in Britain, 1975', *Economic Journal*, vol. 89, 261–79.

——, 1979a, *Poverty and the Impact of Income Maintenance Programmes*, Geneva: International Labour Office.

Besley, T., 1990, 'Means testing versus universal provision in poverty alleviation', *Economica*, vol. 57, 119–29.

—— and Coate, S., 1992, 'Workfare vs. welfare: incentive arguments for work requirements in poverty alleviation programs', *American Economic Review*, vol. 82, 249–61.

Beveridge, W. M. (Lord), 1942, *Social Insurance and Allied Services*, Cmd 6404, London: HMSO.

Blank, R. M., 1993, 'Why were Poverty Rates so High in the 1980s?', in Papadimitriou, D. B., and Wolff, E. N. (eds), *Poverty and Prosperity in the USA in the Late Twentieth Century*, Basingstoke: Macmillan.

——, and Blinder, A. S., 1986, 'Macroeconomics, Income Distribution, and Poverty', in Danziger, S. H., and Weinberg, D. H. (eds), *Fighting Poverty*, Cambridge, Massachusetts: Harvard University Press.

Blundell, R. and Preston, I, 1995, 'Income, expenditure and the living standards of UK households', *Fiscal Studies*, vol. 16, 40–54.

Booth, A. L., 1995, *The Economics of the Trade Union*, Cambridge: Cambridge University Press.

Bourguignon, F. and Fields, G. S., 1990, 'Poverty measures and anti-poverty policy', *Recherches Economiques de Louvain*, vol. 56, 409–27.

—— and Martinez, M., 1996, 'Decomposition of the change in the distribution of primary family incomes: a microsimulation approach applied to France, 1979–1989', Discussion Paper, DELTA, Paris.

Bradshaw, J. and Chen, J.-R., 1996, 'Poverty in the UK: A Comparison with Nineteen Other Countries', Luxembourg Income Study Working Paper No. 147, CEPS/INSTEAD.

Brandolini, A., 1993, 'A description and an assessment of the sample surveys of the personal distribution of incomes in Italy', Microsimulation Unit Discussion Paper 9303, University of Cambridge.

Buhmann, B., Rainwater, L., Schmaus, G., and Smeeding, T., 1988, 'Equivalence Scales, Well-Being, Inequality and Poverty: Sensitivity Estimates Across Ten Countries Using the Luxembourg Income Study (LIS) Database', *Review of Income and Wealth*, vol. 34, 115–42.

Burkhauser, R. V., Smeeding, T. M., and Merz, J., 1996, 'Relative Inequality and Poverty in Germany and the United States Using

Alternative Equivalence Scales', *Review of Income and Wealth*, vol. 42, 381–400.

Burns, P., Crawford, I., and Dilnot, A., 1995, 'Regulation and redistribution in utilities', *Fiscal Studies*, vol. 16, No. 4, 1–22.

Cairncross, A. K., 1958, 'Economic schizophrenia', *Scottish Journal of Political Economy*, vol. 5, 15–21.

Callan, T. and Nolan, B., 1991, 'Concepts of poverty and the poverty line: a critical survey of approaches to measuring poverty', *Journal of Economic Surveys*, vol. 5, 243–62.

——, Nolan, B., Whelan, B. J., Hannan, D. F., with Creighton, S., 1989, *Poverty, Income and Welfare in Ireland*, Paper No 146, Dublin: ESRI.

——, Nolan, B., Whelan, C. T., 1993, 'Resources, Deprivation and the Measurement of Poverty', *Journal of Social Policy*, vol. 22, 141–72.

——, Nolan, B., Whelan, B. J., Whelan, C. T. and Williams, J, 1996, *Poverty in the 1990s*, Dublin: Oak Tree Press.

——, O'Neill, C. J., and O'Donoghue, C., 1995, *Supplementing Family Income*, Paper No. 23, Policy Research Series, ESRI, Dublin.

Cannari, L. and Franco, D., 1997, 'La povertà tra i minorenni in Italia: dimensioni, caratteristiche, politiche', *Temi di discussione*, Numero 294, Rome: Banca D'Italia.

Cantillon, B., 1992, 'De "zero-sum-crisis": een verklaring voor de stabiliteit van de inkomens- en welvaarts-verdeling in periode van economische crisis', *Maandschrift Economie*, vol. 56, 57–73.

——, Marx, I., Proost, D., and Van Dam, R., 1994, *Indicateurs Sociaux: 1985–1992*, Centrum voor Sociaal Beleid, University of Antwerp.

Cantó-Sânchez, O., 1996, 'Poverty Dynamics in Spain: A Study of Transitions in the 1990s', Distributional Analysis Research Programme, Discussion Paper 15, London School of Economics.

CERC, 1989, *Les Français et leurs revenus: le tournant des années 80*, Paris: La Documentation Française.

Citro, C. F. and Michael, R. T., 1995, *Measuring Poverty: A New Approach*, Washington, D.C.: National Academy Press.

Commissione di indagine sulla povertà e sull'emarginazione, 1996, *La Povertà in Italia 1980–1994*, Rome: Presidenza del Consiglio dei Ministri.

——, 1996a, *La Povertà in Italia 1995*, Rome: Presidenza del Consiglio dei Ministri.

Coulter, F., Cowell, F. A, and Jenkins, S. P., 1992, 'Equivalence Scale Relativities and the Extent of Inequality and Poverty', *Economic Journal*, vol. 102, 1067–82.

Cowell, F. A., 1990, *Cheating the Government*, Cambridge, Massachusetts: MIT Press.

—— and Victoria-Feser, M-P, 1996, 'Poverty measurement with contaminated data: a robust approach', *European Economic Review*, vol. 40, 1761–71.

Crijns, L. H. J., 1991, *The EC and Social Security*, Maastricht: European Institute of Public Administration.

Cutler, D. M. and Katz, L. F., 1992, 'Rising inequality? Changes in the distribution of income and consumption in the 1980's', *American Economic Review*, Papers and Proceedings, vol. 82, 546–51.

da Costa, A., 1994, 'The measurement of poverty in Portugal', *Journal of European Social Policy*, vol. 4, 95–115.

De Donder, P. and Hindriks, J., 1996, 'The Political Economy of Targeting', Namur: Facultés N-D de la Paix.

Déchaux, J.-H., 1990, 'Pauvretés ancienne et nouvelle en France', *Observations et Diagnostics Economiques, Revue de l'OFCE*, vol. 33, 1–28.

Deleeck, H., Van den Bosch, K. and Lathouwer L., 1992, *Poverty and the Adequacy of Social Security in the EC*, Aldershot: Avebury.

Department of Health and Social Security, 1975, *Two-Parent Families in Receipt of Family Income Supplement 1972*, London: Statistical and Research Report Series, No. 9.

——, 1988, *Low Income Statistics: Report of a Technical Review*, London: Government Statistical Service.

——, 1988a, *Low Income Families, 1985*, London: Government Statistical Service.

——, 1988b, *Households Below Average Income: A Statistical Analysis 1981–85*, London: Government Statistical Service.

Department of Social Security, 1989, 'Benefit levels and minimum income', House of Commons Social Services Committee, *Minimum Income*, London: HMSO.

——, 1989a, *Social Security Statistics*, London: HMSO.

——, 1991, *Households Below Average Income: Stocktaking*, London: Department of Social Security.

——, 1992, *Households Below Average Income: A Statistical Analysis 1979–1988/89*, London: HMSO.

——, 1993, *Households Below Average Income: A Statistical Analysis 1979–1990/91*, London: HMSO.

——, 1993a, *Income Related Benefits Estimates of Take-Up in 1989*, London: Government Statistical Service.

——, 1993b, *Social Security: The Government's expenditure plans 1993–94 to 1995–96*, Cm 2213, London: HMSO.

——, 1994, *Households Below Average Income: A Statistical Analysis 1979–1991/92*, London: HMSO.

——, 1995, *Households Below Average Income: A Statistical Analysis 1979–1992/93*, London: HMSO.

REFERENCES

——, 1996, *Households Below Average Income: A Statistical Analysis 1979–1993/94*, London: HMSO.

——, 1996a, *Income Related Benefits Estimates of Take-Up in 1994/95*, London: Government Statistical Service.

Desai. M. and Shah, A., 1988, 'An econometric approach to the measurement of poverty', *Oxford Economic Papers*, vol. 40, 505–22.

de Vos, K., 1991, *Micro-Economic Definitions of Poverty*, Rotterdam: Erasmus University.

——, and Garner, T. I., 1991, 'An evaluation of subjective poverty definitions: comparing results from the U.S. and the Netherlands', *Review of Income and Wealth*, vol. 37, 267–85.

de Vos, K. and Zaidi, A., 1995, 'Trend analysis of poverty in the European Community', Rotterdam: Erasmus University, and Tilburg: Economics Institute.

——, ——, 1995a, 'Equivalence scale sensitivity of poverty statistics for the member states of the European Community', Tilburg: Economics Institute.

——, ——, 1996, 'Poverty measurement in the European Union Country-Specific or Union-Wide Poverty Lines', Tilburg: Economics Institute.

Dickens, R., Machin, S. and Manning, A., 1994, 'The effect of minimum wages on employment: theory and evidence from Britain', Centre for Economic Performance Discussion Paper No. 183, LSE.

Dilnot, A. W. and Kell, M., 1987, 'Male unemployment and women's work', *Fiscal Studies*, vol. 8, 1–16.

Dirven, H.-J. and Berghman, J., 1992, 'The evolution of income poverty in the Netherlands', Tilburg: IVA Institute for Social Research.

Drèze, J. H. and Malinvaud E., 1994, 'Growth and employment: the scope for a European initiative', *European Economy*, No. 1, 77–106.

Duclos, J.-Y., 1995, 'Modelling the take-up of state support', *Journal of Public Economics*, vol. 58, 391–415.

——, 1997, 'Estimating and Testing a Model of Welfare Participation: the Case of Supplementary Benefits in Britain', *Economica*, vol. 64, 81–100.

—— and Mercader, M., 1994, 'Household composition and classes of equivalence scales: with application to Spain and the UK', Microsimulation Unit Working Paper MU 94–03, Cambridge: Department of Applied Economics.

Eardley, T., Bradshaw, J., Ditch, J., Gough I. and Whiteford, P., 1996, *Social Assistance in OECD Countries*, Department of Social Security Research Report No. 47, Volumes I and II, London: HMSO.

[164]

Ermisch, J, 1991, 'European integration and external constraints on social policy: is a Social Charter necessary?', *National Institute Economic Review*, May, 93–108.

European Commission, 1981, *Final Report on the First Programme of Pilot Schemes and Studies to Combat Poverty*, Brussels: COM(81), 769 (final).

——, 1989, *Interim Report on the Second European Poverty Programme*, Social Europe, Supplement 2/89.

——, 1991, *Final Report on the Second European Poverty Programme 1985–1989*, Brussels.

Eurostat, 1990, 'Inequality and Poverty in Europe (1980–1985)', *Rapid reports, Population and social conditions*, No 7.

——, 1997 'Income distribution and poverty in EU12 – 1993', *Statistics in Focus*, No 6.

Faure, J. L., 1989 (rapporteur), 'Système statistique sur la pauvreté-précarité', Paris: CNIS.

Fields, G. S., 1980, *Poverty, Inequality, and development*, Cambridge: Cambridge University Press.

Fisher, J. D., Nadler, A. and Whitcher-Alanga, S., 1982, 'Recipient reactions to aid: a conceptual review', *Psychological Bulletin*, vol. 91, 27–59.

Fondation Roi Baudouin, 1994, *Rapport Général sur la Pauvreté*, Pauwels S.A., Eeklo.

Förster, M., 1993, 'Comparing Poverty in 13 OECD Countries – Traditional and Synthetic Approaches', Luxembourg Income Study Working Paper No. 100, CEPS/INSTEAD.

——, 1994, 'The Effects of Net Transfers on Low Incomes among Non-Elderly Families', *OECD Economic Studies*, No. 22, 181–221.

Foster, J. E., Greer, J. and Thorbecke, E., 1984, 'A Class of Decomposable Poverty Measures', *Econometrica*, vol. 52, 761–66.

Fry, V. and Stark, G., 1987, 'The take-up of supplementary benefit: gaps in the "safety net"?', *Fiscal Studies*, vol. 8, 1–14.

Fuchs, V., 1965, 'Towards a theory of poverty' in *The Concept of Poverty*, Washington, D.C.: Chamber of Commerce of the United States, Washington.

Gabszewicz, J. J. and Thisse J.-F., 1979, 'Price competition, quality and income disparities', *Journal of Economic Theory*, vol. 20, 340–59.

Gabszewicz, J. J., Shaked, A., Sutton, J. and Thisse, J.-F., 1986, 'Segmenting the market: the monopolist's optimal product mix', *Journal of Economic Theory*, vol. 39, 273–89.

Gannon, T. M. S. J., 1987, *The Catholic Challenge to the American Economy*, New York: Macmillan.

Gardiner, K., Hills, J., Falkingham, J., Lechene, V., and Sutherland,

H., 1995, 'The effects of differences in housing and health care systems on international comparisons of income distribution', Welfare State Programme Discussion Paper No. 110, London School of Economics.

Gillis., M., Jenkins, G. and Leitzel, J., 1986, 'Financing universal access in the telephone network', *National Tax Journal*, vol. 39, 35–48.

Goedhart, T., Halberstadt, V., Kapteyn, A. and van Praag, B., 1977, 'The poverty line: concept and measurement', *Journal of Human Resources*, vol. 12: 503–20.

Goodin, R. E., 1985, 'Erring on the side of kindness in social welfare policy', *Policy Sciences*, vol. 18, 141–56.

Goodin, R. E., 1988, *Reasons for Welfare*, Princeton: Prineton University Press.

Goodman, A., Johnson, P. and Webb, S., 1997, *Inequality in the UK*, Oxford: Oxford University Press.

—— and Webb, S., 1994, *For Richer, For Poorer*, IFS Commentary No. 42, London: IFS.

——, 1995, 'The distribution of UK household expenditure, 1979–92', *Fiscal Studies*, vol. 16, 55–80.

——, 1995a, *The Distribution of UK Household Expenditure, 1979–92*, IFS Commentary No. 49, London: IFS.

Gorman, W. M., 1956, 'A possible procedure for analyzing quality differentials in the egg market', Mimeo: Iowa State College. (reissued as Discussion Paper No. B4 of the London School of Economics Econometrics Programme).

Gramlich, E. M., 1974, ' The Distributional Effects of Higher Unemployment', *Brookings Papers on Economic Activity*, 2, 293–336.

Gregg, P., and Wadsworth, J., 1996, 'More work in fewer households?', in Hills, J., editor, *New Inequalities*, Cambridge: Cambridge University Press.

Gustafsson, B. and Uusitalo, H., 1990, 'The welfare state and poverty in Finland and Sweden from the mid-1960s to the mid-1980s', *Review of Income and Wealth*, series 36, 249–66.

Haddad, L. and Kanbur, R., 1990, 'How serious is the neglect of intra-household inequality?', *Economic Journal*, vol. 100, 866–81.

Hagenaars, A., de Vos, K. and Zaidi, A., 1994, *Poverty Statistics in the late 1980s*, Luxembourg: Eurostat.

Hahn, F. H. and Matthews, R. C. O., 1964, 'The theory of economic growth', *Economic Journal*, vol. 74, 779–902.

Halleröd, B., 1995, 'The truly poor: direct and indirect consensual measurement of poverty in Sweden', *Journal of European Social Policy*, vol. 5, 111–29.

——, Heikkilä, M., Mäntysaari, M., Ritakallio, V.-M., and Nyman, C., 1996, 'The Nordic Countries: Poverty in a Welfare State' in

Øyen, E, Miller, S. M. and Samad, S. A. (eds), *Poverty: A Global Review*, Oslo: Scandinavian University Press.

Hancock, R., and Waddams Price, C., 1995, 'Competition in the British domestic gas market: efficiency and equity', *Fiscal Studies*, vol. 16, no. 3, 81–105.

Hansen, H. and Hultin, M. L., 1997, *Actual and Potential Recipients of Welfare Benefits with a Focus on Housing Benefits, 1987–1992*, Copenhagen: The Rockwool Foundation Research Unit Study No. 4.

Harris, G., 1994, *The Take-Up of Income-Related Benefits*, Analytical Notes No. 3, London: Department of Social Security.

Hauser, R., 1996, 'Vergleichende Analyse der Einkommensverteilung und der Einkommensarmut in den alten und neuen Bundesländern von 1990 bis 1995' in Becker, I. and Hauser, R., 'Einkommensverteilung und Armut in Deutschland von 1962 bis 1995', Arbeitspapier Nr 9, EVS-Projekt, Universität Frankfurt am Main.

—— and Semrau, P., 1989, 'Trends in poverty and low income in the Federal Republic of Germany', Working Paper No 306, Sonderforschungsbereich 3, University of Frankfurt.

—— ——, 1990, *Poverty in the Federal Republic of Germany*, report prepared for the European Commission.

Hausman, P., 1995, 'Le revenu des ménages', Document PSELL No. 77, Walferdange, Luxembourg: CEPS/Instead.

Haveman, R. H., 1987, *Poverty Policy and Poverty Research*, Madison: University of Wisconsin Press.

Hayek, F. A., 1960, *The Constitution of Liberty*, London: Routledge Kegan Paul.

Herrero, C., 1995, 'Capabilities and Utilities', Working paper AD 95–06, University of Alicante: IVIE.

Hirschman, A. O., 1970, *Exit, Voice and Loyalty*, Cambridge, Massachusetts: Harvard University Press.

HM Treasury, 1988, *The Government's Expenditure Plans 1988–89 to 1990–91*, London: HMSO.

International Labour Office, 1984, *Into the Twenty-First Century: the Development of Social Security*, Geneva: ILO.

Jallade, J.-P., 1988, 'Redistribution in the Welfare State: an assessment of the French performance' in Jallade, J-P, editor, *The Crisis of Redistribution in European Welfare States*, Stoke on Trent: Trentham Books.

Jäntti, M., 1992, 'Poverty Dominance and Statistical Inference', Research Report 1992:7, Stockholm University: Department of Statistics.

—— and Ritakallio, V.-M., 1996, 'Ekonomisk fattigdom i Finland åren 1971 till 1993', in Nordisk Ministerråd, 1996, *Den nordiska fattigdomens utveckling och struktur*, Copenhagen: Tema-Nord.

Jenkins, S. P., 1991, 'Poverty Measurement and the Within-Household Distribution: Agenda for Action', *Journal of Social Policy*, vol. 20, 457–83.

—— and Cowell, F. A., 1994, 'Parametric equivalence scales and scale relativities', *Economic Journal*, vol. 104, 891–900.

Johnson, P. and Webb, S., 1989, 'Counting people on low incomes: the effect of recent changes in official statistics', *Fiscal Studies*, vol. 10.

——, ——, 1990, *Poverty in Official Statistics: Two Reports*, London: IFS Commentary No. 24.

——, ——, 1991, *UK Poverty Statistics: A Comparative Study*, London: IFS Commentary No. 27.

Kakwani, N., 1993, 'Statistical Inference in the Measurement of Poverty', *Review of Economics and Statistics*, vol. 75, 632–39.

Kanbur, R., 1987, 'Measurement and alleviation of poverty', *IMF Staff Papers*, vol. 34, 60–85.

——, Keen, M. and Tuomala, M., 1990, 'Optimal non-linear income taxation for the alleviation of income poverty', IFS Discussion Paper 91/2.

Kangas, O. and Ritakallio, V.-M., 1995, 'Different methods – Different results?: Approaches to Multidimensional Poverty', University of Pavia: Paper presented at the ISA RC 19 Conference, 14–17 September 1995.

Kapteyn, A., Kooreman, P. and Willense, R., 1987, 'Some methodological issues in the implementation of subjective poverty definitions', Research Memorandum FEW 245, Tilburg University: Department of Econometrics.

Kay, J. A., Keen, M. J., and Morris, C. N., 1984, 'Estimating consumption from expenditure data', *Journal of Public Economics*, vol. 23, 169–81.

Kilpatrick, R. W., 1973, 'The income elasticity of the poverty line', *Review of Economics and Statistics*, vol. 55, 327–32.

Lampman, R. J., 1971, *Ends and Means of Reducing Income Poverty*, Chicago: Markham.

Lancaster, K., 1966, 'A new approach to consumer theory', *Journal of Political Economy*, vol. 74, 132–57.

Layard, R., Nickell, S., and Jackman, R., 1991, *Unemployment*, Oxford: Oxford University Press.

Lewis, G. W. and Ulph, D. T., 1988, 'Poverty, inequality and welfare', *Economic Journal*, vol. 98, conference issue, 117–31.

Lindbeck, A., 1992, 'Macroeconomic theory and the labor market', *European Economic Review*, vol. 36, 209–35.

——, 1993, *Unemployment and Macroeconomics*, Cambridge, Massachusetts: MIT Press.

——, 1995, 'Hazardous Welfare-State dynamics', *American Economic*

Review, Papers and Proceedings, vol. 85, 9–15.

Lollivier, S. and Verger, D., 1997, 'Une approche de la pauvreté par les conditions de vie: le cas français', Le Mans: paper presented at AFSE Meeting, 13–14 May 1997.

Lovell, C. A. K., Richardson, S., Travers, P. and Wood, L., 1990, 'Resources and Functionings: A New View of Inequality in Australia', Working paper 90–7, University of Adelaide: Department of Economics.

Low Income Project Team, 1996, *Low income, food, nutrition and health: strategies for improvement*, London: Department of Health.

Lynes, T., 1967, *French Pensions*, London: Bell.

Mack, J. and Lansley, S., 1985, *Poor Britain*, London: Allen and Unwin.

Mankiw, N. G., 1994, *Macroeconomics*, second edition, New York: Worth Publishers.

Marsh, A. and McKay, S., 1993, *Families, Work and Benefits*, London: PSI.

Martinetti, E. C., 1996, 'Standard of Living Evaluation Based on Sen's Approach: Some Methodological Suggestions', *Notizie di Politeia*, vol. 12, 37–53.

McGregor, P. L. and V. K. Borooah, 1992, 'Is Low Spending or Low Income a Better Indicator of Whether or Not a Household is Poor: Some Results from the 1985 Family Expenditure Survey', *Journal of Social Policy*, vol. 21, 53–69.

Meade, J. E., 1991, *The Building of the New Europe: National Diversity versus Continental Uniformity*, Edinburgh: Hume Occasional Papers No. 28.

Mercader-Prats, M., 1993, 'The Low Income Population in Spain and a comparison with France and the UK', Welfare State Programme Discussion Paper 95, LSE

——, 1997, 'Identifying Low Standards of Living: Evidence from Spain', Working Paper 97.02, Universitat Autònoma de Barcelona: Department d'Economia Aplicada.

Meulders, D., Joyeux, C., and Plasman, R., 1996, 'Poverty in Belgium', Charleston: paper presented at World Congress of Social Economics.

Meulemans, M. and Marannes, F., 1993, 'La répartition des revenus du patrimoine', *Cahiers Economiques de Bruxelles*, No 137, 318–52.

Ministry of Pensions and National Insurance, 1966, *Financial and other circumstances of Retirement Pensioners*, London: HMSO.

Mirrlees, J. A., 1971, 'An exploration in the theory of optimum income taxation', *Review of Economic Studies*, vol. 38, 175–208.

Missoc, 1996, *Social Protection in the Member States of the Union*, Brussels: DG-V.

Muellbauer, J. N. J., 1974, 'Prices and inequality: the United Kingdom experience', *Economic Journal*, vol. 84, 32–55.

Muffels, R., Kapteyn, A. and Berghman, J., 1990, *Poverty in the Netherlands*, 's-Gravenhage: VUGA.

Murphy, D., 1984, 'The Impact of State Taxes and Benefits on Irish Household Incomes', *Journal of the Statistical and Social Inquiry Society of Ireland*, vol. 25, 55–120.

National Anti-Poverty Strategy, 1997, *Sharing in Progress*, Dublin: Stationery Office.

Nolan, B., 1996, 'Income Inequality and Poverty in Ireland 1987–94: Aggregate Results and Trends', Dublin: ESRI.

Nolan, B. and Callan, T., 1994, editors, *Poverty and Policy in Ireland*, Dublin: Gill and Macmillan.

—— and Whelan, C. T., 1996, *Resources, Deprivation, and Poverty*, Oxford: Clarendon Press.

—— and Whelan, C. T., 1996a, 'Measuring poverty using income and deprivation indicators: alternative approaches', *Journal of European Social Policy*, vol. 6, 225–40.

Nordisk Ministerråd, 1996, *Den nordiska fattigdomens utveckling och struktur*, Copenhagen: Tema-Nord.

O'Higgins, M. and Jenkins, S., 1990, 'Poverty in Europe: Estimates for 1975, 1980 and 1985', *Analyzing Poverty in the European Community*, Luxembourg: Eurostat News Special Edition, 1–1990.

OECD, 1982, *Social Indicators*, Paris: OECD.

——, 1982a, *The Challenge of Unemployment*, Paris: OECD.

——, 1995, *Historical Statistics 1960–1993*, Paris: OECD.

Oi, W., 1971, 'A Disneyland dilemma: two-part tariffs for a Mickey Mouse monopoly', *Quarterly Journal of Economics*, vol. 85, 77–96.

Orshansky, M., 1965, 'Counting the Poor: Another Look at the Poverty Profile', *Social Security Bulletin*, vol. 28, pp. 3–29.

Øyen, E., Miller, S. M. and Samad, S. A., editors, 1996, *Poverty: A Global Review*, Oslo: Scandinavian University Press.

Parker, H., 1989, *Instead of the Dole*, London: Routledge.

Paugam, S., 1996, *l'exclusion: l'état des savoirs*, Paris: la découverte.

Pauly, M., 1973, 'Income redistribution as a local public good', *Journal of Public Economics*, vol. 2, 35–58.

Persson, T. and Tabellini, G., 1990, *Macroeconomic Policy, Credibility and Politics*, New York: Harwood.

Peterson, P. E and Rom, M C, 1990, *Welfare Magnets*, Washington, D.C.: Brookings Institution.

Petmesidou, M., 1996, 'Greece, Turkey, and Cyprus: Poverty Research in a Policy Vacuum' in Øyen, E., Miller, S. M. and Samad, S. A. (eds), *Poverty: A Global Review*, Oslo: Scandinavian University Press.

Petty, Sir William, 1676, *The Economic Writings of Sir William Petty*, Hull, C. (ed.), New York: reprinted by A. M. Kelley, 1964.

Piachaud, D. and Webb, J., 1996, *The price of food*, STICERD Occasional Paper 20, LSE.

Pissarides, C., 1991, 'Macroeconomic adjustment and poverty in selected developed countries', *World Bank Economic Review*, vol. 5, 207–29.

Preston, I., 1993, 'Large and small sample distribution of relative poverty statistics', Working Paper W93/22, London: Institute for Fiscal Studies.

Pryke, R., 1995, *Taking the Measure of Poverty*, London: Institute of Economic Affairs.

Quintin, Q., 1989, 'The Commission's political conclusions', Windsor: European Conference on Basic Income.

Ramprakash., D., 1994, 'Poverty in the countries of the European Union: A Synthesis of Eurostat's statistical research on poverty', *Journal of European Social Policy*, vol. 4, 117–28.

Ravallion, M., 1992, *Poverty Comparisons: A Guide to Concepts and Methods*, Washington, D.C.: The World Bank.

——, 1994, 'Measuring Social Welfare With and Without Poverty Lines', *American Economic Review*, Papers and Proceedings, vol. 84, 359–64.

—— and Chao, K., 1989, 'Targeted policies for poverty alleviation under imperfect information: algorithms and applications', *Journal of Policy Modeling*, Vol. 11, 213–24.

Rawls, J., 1971, *A Theory of Justice*, Cambridge, Massachusetts: Harvard University Press.

Ribich, T., 1968, *Education and Poverty*, Washington, D.C.: Brookings Institution.

Ritakallio, V.-M., 1994, 'Finnish poverty: a cross-national comparison', LIS Working Paper No. 119.

Rowntree, B. S., 1901, *Poverty: A Study of Town Life*, London: Longmans, Green and Co. (new edition, 1922).

——, 1941, *Poverty and Progress*, London: Longmans, Green and Co.

—— and Lavers, G. R., 1951, *Poverty and the Welfare State*, London: Longmans.

Ruiz-Castillo, J., 1987, *La Medición de la Pobreza y de la Desigualdad en España, 1980–81*, Estudios Económicos, Banco de España, No. 42.

Saunders, P., 1997, 'The meaning of poverty', *SPRC Newsletter*, No 65, Social Policy Research Centre, Sydney: University of New South Wales.

Schokkaert, E. and Van Ootegen, E., 1990, 'Sen's Concept of Living Standard Applied to the Belgian Unemployed', *Recherches Economiques de Louvain*, vol. 56, 429–50.

Scholz, J. K., 1994, 'The Earned Income Tax Credit: participation, compliance, and antipoverty effectiveness', *National Tax Journal*, vol. 47, 63–87.

Schweinitz, K. de, 1943, *England's Road to Social Security*, Philadelphia: University of Pennsylvania Press.

Seidl, C., 1994, 'How sensible is the Leyden individual welfare function of income?', *European Economic Review*, vol. 38, 1633–59.

Seidman, L. S., 1990, *Saving for America's Economic Future*, New York: Sharpe, Armonk.

Sen, A. K., 1974, 'Informational bases of alternative welfare approaches, *Journal of Public Economics*, vol. 3, 387–403.

——, 1976, 'Poverty: an ordinal approach to measurement', *Econometrica*, vol. 44, 219–31.

——, 1983, 'Poor, relatively speaking', *Oxford Economic Papers*, vol. 35, 153–69; reprinted in Sen (1984).

——, 1984, *Resources, Values and Development*, Cambridge, Massachusetts: Harvard University Press.

——, 1985, *Commodities and Capabilities*, Amsterdam: North Holland.

——, 1988, 'Freedom of choice: concept and content', *European Economic Review*, vol. 32, 269–94.

——, 1992, *Inequality Re-Examined*, Cambridge, Massachusetts: Harvard University Press.

——, 1997, 'Inequality, Unemployment and Contemporary Europe', Development Economics Research Programme Discussion Paper, London School of Economics.

—— and Foster, J., 1997, *On Economic Inequality*, second edition, Oxford: Clarendon Press.

Shaked, A. and Sutton, J., 1982, 'Relaxing Price Competition through Product Differentiation', *Review of Economic Studies*, vol. 49, 3–13.

——, ——, 1983, 'Natural Oligopolies', *Econometrica*, vol. 51, 1469–83.

Shorrocks, A. F., 1995, 'Revisiting the Sen poverty index', *Econometrica*, vol. 63, 1225–30.

Silva, M., 1992, 'Child poverty and deprivation in Portugal', Innocenti Occasional Papers, Economic Policy Series, Number 28, Florence: UNICEF.

Silver, H., 1995, 'Reconceptualizing social disadvantage: Three paradigms of social exclusion', in Rodgers, G., Gore, C. and Figueiredo, J. B. (eds), *Social Exclusion: Rhetoric, Realtiy, Responses*, Geneva: ILO.

Sinn, H.-W., 1990, 'Tax harmonisation or tax competition in Europe?', *European Economic Review*, vol. 34, 489–504.

Slesnick, D. T., 1993, 'Gaining Ground: Poverty in the Postwar United States', *Journal of Political Economy*, vol. 101, 1–38.

REFERENCES

Smeeding, T., Saunders, P., Coder, J., Jenkins, S., Fritzell, J., Hagenaars, A. J. M., Hauser, R. and Wolfson, M., 1993, 'Poverty, Inequality, and Family Living Standards Impacts Across Seven Nations: The Effects of Noncash Subsidies for Health, Education and Housing', *Review of Income and Wealth*, vol. 39, 229–56.

Stevens, C., 1973, *Public Assistance in France*, London: Bell.

Stewart, F., 1996, 'Basic Needs, Capabilities, and Human Development', in A. Offer (ed.), *In Pursuit of the Quality of Life*, Oxford: Oxford University Press.

Strobel, P., 1996, 'From poverty to exclusion', *International Social Science Journal*, 148, 173–89.

Sugden, R., 1993, 'Welfare, Resources, and Capabilities: A Review of *Inequality Reexamined* by Amartya Sen', *Journal of Economic Literature*, vol. 31, 1947–62.

Sutherland, H., 1996, 'Households, Individuals and the Re-Distribution of Income', Microsimulation Unit Working Paper MU 9601, Cambridge: Department of Applied Economics.

Swedish Ministry of Finance, 1996, *Report on Income Distribution*, Stockholm: Cabinet Office.

Synthèses, 1995, No. 1, *Revenus et Patrimoine des Ménages*, Paris: INSEE.

——, 1996, No. 5, *Revenus et Patrimoine des Ménages*, Paris: INSEE.

Tinbergen, J., 1952, *On the Theory of Economic Policy*, Amsterdam: North Holland.

——, 1954, *Centralization and Decentralization in Economic Policy*, Amsterdam: North Holland.

Tirole, J., 1989, *The Theory of Industrial Organization*, Cambridge, Massachusetts: MIT Press.

Tobin, J., 1970, 'Raising the Incomes of the Poor', in K Gordon, editor, *Agenda for the Nation*, Washington D.C.: Brookings Institution.

Townsend, P., 1954, 'Measuring poverty', *British Journal of Sociology*, vol. 5, 130–7.

——, 1962, 'The meaning of poverty', *British Journal of Sociology*, vol. 13, 210–27.

——, 1979, *Poverty in the United Kingdom*, Harmondsworth: Allen Lane.

——, 1990, *The Poor Are Poorer: A Statistical Report on Changes in the Living Standards of Rich and Poor in the United Kingdom 1979–1989*, University of Bristol: Statistical Monitoring Unit.

——, 1993, *The International Analysis of Poverty*, Hemel Hempstead: Harvester Wheatsheaf.

Travers, P., 1996, 'Deprivation Among Low Income DSS Australian Families: Results from a Pilot Study', in R. Thanki and C. Thomson (eds), *Mortgaging Our Future? Families and Young People in Aus-*

tralia, SPRC Reports and Proceedings No 129, Social Policy Research Centre, Sydney: University of New South Wales.

Tsakloglou, P., 1990, 'Aspects of Poverty in Greece', *Review of Income and Wealth*, vol. 36, 381–402.

Uusitalo, H., 1989, *Income Distribution in Finland*, Helsinki: Central Statistical Office of Finland.

Van den Bosch, K. with Marx, I., 1996, 'Trends in Financial Poverty in OECD Countries', Luxembourg Income Study Working Paper No 148, CEPS/INSTEAD.

——, Callan, T., Estivill, J., Hausman, P., Jeandidier, B., Muffels, R. and Yfantopoulos, J., 1993, 'A comparison of poverty in seven European countries and regions using subjective and relative measures', *Journal of Population Economics*, vol. 6, 235–59.

van Oorschot, W., 1991, 'Non-take-up of social security benefits in Europe', *Journal of European Social Policy*, vol. 1, 15–30.

Van Parijs, P., 1991, 'Why surfers should be fed: The liberal case for an unconditional basic income', *Philosophy and Public Affairs*, vol. 20, 101–31.

van Praag, B. M. S., Hagenaars, A. J. and van Weeren, H., 1982, 'Poverty in Europe', *Review of Income and Wealth*, vol. 28, 345–59.

——, and Kapteyn, A., 1994, 'How sensible is the Leyden individual welfare function of income? A Reply', *European Economic Review*, vol. 38, 1817–25.

Vickers, J., 1997, 'Regulation, Competition, and the Structure of Prices', *Oxford Review of Economic Policy*, vol. 13, no. 1, 15–26.

Vickrey, C., 1977, 'The time-poor: a new look at poverty', *Journal of Human Resources*, vol. 12, 27–48.

von Tunzelmann, G. N., 1995, 'Time-Saving Technical Change: The Cotton Industry in the English Industrial Revolution', *Explorations in Economic History*, vol. 32, 1–27.

Watts, H. W., 1968, 'An economic definition of poverty' in D. P. Moynihan (ed.), *On Understanding Poverty*, New York: Basic Books.

Weinberg, A. and Ruano-Borbalan, J.-C., 1993, 'Comprendre l'exclusion', *Sciences Humaines*, vol. 28, 12–15.

Weisbrod, B. A., 1970, 'Collective action and the distribution of income: a conceptual approach' in R. H. Haveman and J. Margolis (eds), *Public Expenditure and Policy Analysis*, Chicago: Markham.

Weiss, A., 1990, *Efficiency Wages*, Chur: Harwood.

Whiteford, P., 1985, *A Family's Needs: Equivalence Scales, Poverty and Social Security*, Department of Social Security Research Paper no. 27, Canberra: Government Printer.

Whittle, C., 1977, 'Social assistance in the Federal Republic of Germany', London: Department of Health and Social Security.

——, 1978, 'Social assistance in France', London: Department of Health and Social Security.

World Bank, 1996, *World Development Report 1996*, Oxford: Oxford University Press.

Zaidi, A. and de Vos, K., 1996, 'Trends in consumption-based poverty and inequality in the Member States of the European Community', Lillehammer: paper presented at 24th General Conference of the International Association of Research on Income and Wealth.

Zetterberg, S., 1984, *Yrjö and Hilma Jahnsson*, Helsinki: The Yrjö Jahnsson Foundation.

Index

Note that in the case of publications with more than one author or editor, only the first persons listed are named in the body of the text or in the footnotes. The Index, however, also contains page references for co-editors or co-authors not directly mentioned. Full publication details are provided in the References.